Toronto Sketches 12

# MIKE FILEY

# Toronto
# Sketches
12

DUNDURN
TORONTO

Unless otherwise noted, all photos are from the Mike Filey collection.

Project Editor: Jennifer McKnight
Copy Editor: Andrea Waters
Design: Laura Boyle
Cover Design: Courtney Horner
Front Cover Illustration: Mike Filey Collection
Author Photo: Courtesy of John McQuarrie
Printer: Webcom

**Library and Archives Canada Cataloguing in Publication**

Filey, Mike, 1941-, author
  Toronto sketches 12 : "the way we were" / Mike Filey.

(Toronto sketches ; 12)
"The way we were" columns from the Toronto Sunday Sun.
Issued in print and electronic formats.
ISBN 978-1-4597-3169-1 (pbk.).--ISBN 978-1-4597-3171-4 (epub).-- ISBN 978-1-4597-3170-7 (pdf)


1. Toronto (Ont.)--History. I. Title. II. Title: Toronto sketches twelve.

FC3097.4.F54983 2015      971.3'541      C2015-900764-X
                                         C2015-900765-8


1   2   3   4   5       19   18   17   16   15

 Conseil des Arts du Canada / Canada Council for the Arts  Canada  ONTARIO ARTS COUNCIL CONSEIL DES ARTS DE L'ONTARIO an Ontario government agency un organisme du gouvernement de l'Ontario

We acknowledge the support of the **Canada Council for the Arts** and the **Ontario Arts Council** for our publishing program. We also acknowledge the financial support of the **Government of Canada** through the **Canada Book Fund** and **Livres Canada Books**, and the **Government of Ontario** through the **Ontario Book Publishing Tax Credit** and the **Ontario Media Development Corporation.**

Care has been taken to trace the ownership of copyright material used in this book. The author and the publisher welcome any information enabling them to rectify any references or credits in subsequent editions.
— *J. Kirk Howard, President*

The publisher is not responsible for websites or their content unless they are owned by the publisher.

Printed and bound in Canada.

VISIT US AT
Dundurn.com | @dundurnpress | Facebook.com/dundurnpress | Pinterest.com/dundurnpress


Dundurn
3 Church Street, Suite 500
Toronto, Ontario, Canada
M5E 1M2

*This volume of collected works is dedicated to Yarmila, my faithful spell-checker, image manager, typist, and wife of forty-seven years (and in case she reads this, these responsibilities are not in that order).*

# Contents

Publisher's Note                              11

Here's to Our Kennedys                        13

St. Clair Bridge Still Gives Us Trouble       16

Cemetery Last Port of Call                    18

Escaping Summer by Boat                       21

They Lined Up to Cross Niagara                24

Where Is Our Spitfire?                        26

Makin' Tracks Through History                 29

This 1910 Idea Was a Real Lifesaver           32

Pleasant Streetcar History                    35

From Civic to Simcoe                          38

This Canuck Was a Golf God                    41

Toronto Still Yonge at Heart                  44

The Ill-Fated Ex of 1974                      47

CNE's Back to the Future 50

Stately Structures Indeed 53

World's First Movie Star 56

Streamlining T.O.'s Streets 59

Rollin', Rollin' Down the River 62

*Keewatin* Comes Home 65

Tunnel Comes in for Landing 68

Mother Parker Turns One Hundred 71

Belt Line Was Short-Tracked 74

Wharf Lighthouse Turns 150 77

The Very First Grey Cup 79

Travels Back in Time 82

Gardiner in a Pickle 85

T.O.'s Evolving Skyline 88

T.O.'s Little Piece of Venice 91

Identified Flying Object 94

Toronto's Master Sleuth 97

The Best-Laid Plans … 100

T.O. Tried Its Luck Before 103

Starter Motors 106

T.O.'s Second Subway 109

A Real Swinger on Bathurst 113

Gargoyles Get a Second Life 116

The Fileys Head South 118

Historic and Truly Moving     121

Jets Back on Island Radar     124

A Hot Time in the Old Town of York     127

Streetcar Inferno     129

Toronto's Changing Waterfront     132

Floating History     135

Postcard from the Wedge     138

Toronto's Early Hotels     141

The Little Tug That Could     144

Northern Fighters     147

The Way We Kept Our Cool     150

Wonderful Flying Machine     154

Never Got Off the Ground     158

Never Taxed for a Topic     161

Scarborough's Lost Dream     164

Getting There from Here     167

City Joined the Streetcar Biz     170

Toronto's Union Station, Then and Then     173

Toronto's Worst Disaster     176

Can't Beat New City Hall     179

When Vaudeville Ruled     183

Take the Time to Go to Jail     186

Pachyderms from the Past     190

Our First Remembrance     193

First TTC Rider Paid 7¢ Fare     196

Mi Casa Es Su Casa     198

Streetcar's Brush with Fame     202

A Piece of T.O.'s Flying History     206

When Eaton's Was Christmas     209

1944 Storm Still the Worst     212

# Publisher's Note

Mike Filey's column "The Way We Were" has appeared in the *Toronto Sunday Sun* on a regular basis since 1975. Many of his earlier columns have been reproduced in volumes 1 through 11 of Dundurn Press's Toronto Sketches series. The columns in this book originally appeared in 2012 and 2013. Appended to each column is the date it first appeared as well as any relevant material that may have surfaced since that date (indicated by an asterisk).

# Here's to Our Kennedys

## May 6, 2012

What today are acknowledged as two of our city's busiest thorough-fares, Kennedy and Ellesmere roads, began as a couple of dusty pioneer roads in the wilds of what had been established as the Township of Scarborough back in 1850. According to Scarborough archivist Rick Schofield, Kennedy Road was named in recognition of the Kennedy family, many of whom were prominent in the early development of the township. Two of the best known Kennedys were brothers Samuel and William, who owned several hundred-acre farms on the west side of Kennedy north of Sheppard. Other family members farmed on Church Street, a thoroughfare that was subsequently renamed Midland Avenue after the Midland Railway of Canada, an early transportation company that was to become part of the new CNR when the latter was established in 1923. Much of the Midland Railway's original right-of-way through Scarborough still exists between Kennedy and Midland and is used by GO trains on the Stouffville route.

Another prominent member of the pioneer Kennedy family was Lyman Kennedy, who served as Scarborough Township Reeve from 1896 to 1901.

The name Ellesmere was selected for the small community that developed in the early 1800s in and around this same dusty crossroads by settlers who had arrived in the New World from Ellesmere, Shropshire,

Looking north on Kennedy Road over Ellesmere Road in 1912. This image appeared on a postcard published by Henry and Clarence Herington, who worked out of an office in Trenton, Ontario. The brothers photographed and published numerous postcards of small Ontario towns. One of their biggest fans is *Toronto Sun* reporter Ian Robertson, who hopes to write a book about the family one day.

A similar view of the same intersection exactly one hundred years later. Note the slight bend in Kennedy Road, which still exists, possibly a result of a minor miscalculation by the early surveyors.

England. Helen Foster, the archive assistant with the Shropshire council government (great thing, this email and Internet stuff) says that the word *Ellesmere*, or more correctly *Ellesmeles*, dates back to the eleventh century. It's believed that the *Elles* portion of the word refers to a Saxon personal name, while *meles* or *mere* refers to a lake defined as being "broad in relation to its depth."

# St. Clair Bridge Still Gives Us Trouble

## May 20, 2012

For the longest time, the project that saw the upgrading of the TTC's St. Clair streetcar route (which began service in its original form exactly ninety-nine years ago this coming August 15) was the brunt of all sorts of controversy. And while the provincial government's environmental approval of the line was given in June 2005, the streetcars didn't begin operating over the new dedicated right-of-way until the summer of 2010. Though some are still convinced that the project has not been a success, many others are beginning to appreciate what has been accomplished.

But there is still a shortcoming along the seven-kilometre-long route, and that's the railway bridge between Old Weston Road and Keele Street, which continues to result in vehicular traffic congestion. Trains have crossed St. Clair Avenue at this location for more than one hundred years. Because street traffic in the form of horses and wagons was much less back then, a level crossing was sufficient. However, with the arrival of the motor car, combined with the westward expansion of the city, a bridge was the only answer to what was becoming a dangerous situation. Work on the present structure began in April 1931, and on May 14 of the following year the new "subway" (as such structures were known back then), built at a cost of $430,000, was officially opened, allowing the St. Clair streetcars to be extended to Keele Street.

An initial estimate to replace the structurally sound eighty-year-old bridge presents a figure close to $30 million! Now what?

On May 14, 1932, representatives of the TTC and the Canadian National and Canadian Pacific Railways, along with various elected city officials (including Mayor William Stewart, who served from 1931 to 1934 and whose nephew Bill Stewart just retired as Toronto's Fire Chief), join with members of the nearby community to celebrate the official opening of the new "subway" on St. Clair Avenue West. (Photo from the City of Toronto Archives.)

# Cemetery Last Port of Call

## May 27, 2012

Last month, in recognition of the one hundredth anniversary of the April 15, 1912, sinking of the White Star Line's RMS *Titanic* with the loss of more than fifteen hundred lives, television stations, newspapers, magazines, and Internet sites worldwide featured all kinds of stories about the tragic event. For my part I devoted my April 15, 2012, *Sunday Sun* column (one hundred years to the day!) to the three Canadian survivors, Mary and Ethel Gordon and Major Arthur Peuchen, who now lie at rest in Toronto's beautiful Mount Pleasant Cemetery.

The world was shaken by an accident that the experts were sure just couldn't happen, then another enormous marine disaster occurred a little more than two years later when on May 29, 1914, the Canadian Pacific's Atlantic steamer RMS *Empress of Ireland*, bound for Liverpool from the Port of Quebec City with 1,477 passengers and crew, was rammed by the Norwegian coal freighter SS *Storstad* in the St. Lawrence River not far from the town of Rimouski. The *Empress* sank in less than 14 minutes with a loss of 842 passengers and 172 crew members. Of the 842 passengers, 167 were members of the Salvation Army who were on their way to an international conference scheduled to convene in London, England, early in June. Many of those 167 were from Toronto. Two years after the disaster, in 1916, an awe-inspiring memorial to their memory was erected in Mount Pleasant Cemetery.

The caskets of sixteen Salvation Army victims of the RMS *Empress of Ireland* marine disaster were laid to rest in Mount Pleasant Cemetery on June 6, 1914. The total number of "Sally Ann" victims would increase to 167, many of them members of the band of the Toronto Citadel. (Photo from the Salvation Army Archives.)

As has taken place on the Sunday closest to May 29 every year since the sinking, a special service will again be held at the memorial. This year's will commence at 3:00 p.m. and, of course, the public is invited.

As if these two marine disasters in such a short span of time weren't enough, a third sinking of a large passenger ship was to rattle the world's ocean-crossing public less than a year later when the Cunard liner RMS *Lusitania* was torpedoed by a German submarine off Ireland's southern coastline. This time 1,198 on board died. Of those, a total of 76 Canadians lost their lives. One of the last to succumb to the act of violence had actually survived the sinking. Alfred Clarke was president of Canada's top tanning and leather manufacturing business. His large factory was at 633 Eastern Avenue, a site now occupied by Cinespace Film Studios. With war raging in Europe, Clarke was on his way to England to promote his company's various products. That trip was cut short when

Toronto businessman A.R. Clarke's monument in Mount Pleasant Cemetery. Note the reference to his being a victim of the RMS *Lusitania* tragedy.

without warning the ship exploded. Wrapping himself in a life jacket, he threw himself into the cold Atlantic Ocean. After several hours he was discovered floating face upward. Taken ashore, Clarke soon felt well enough to travel and continued on to London by train. But something was not right. In London he proceeded to the famous Fitzroy Hospital, where he was diagnosed with a broken rib and pleurisy. Pneumonia soon followed, and on June 20, some twenty-two days after the sinking, this prominent Canadian was dead. Clarke's remains were removed to Toronto, where he was laid to rest in Mount Pleasant Cemetery. The inscription on his monument reveals to all who pass by that he was "A VICTIM OF THE LUSITANIA."

# Escaping Summer by Boat

## June 3, 2012

During the summers of long ago, the most popular way to get away from the stifling heat of the big city was to take a day trip on one of the many passenger steamers that were moored at the foot of Bay or Yonge streets. After boarding one of the ships with such mysterious-sounding names as *Corona*, *Cibola*, *Chippewa*, or *Cayuga*, it wasn't long before you were in another world enjoying the cool Lake Ontario breezes as you and your fellow travellers headed for the Niagara River ports at Niagara-on-the-Lake or Queenston, or perhaps even the foreign port on the other side of the river at Lewiston in New York State.

But, as someone once said, all good things must come to an end. In the case of these waterfront icons it was due to the arrival of the automobile, and more specifically to the new superhighways like the Queen Elizabeth Way, which allowed families to drive using their own timetables to and from Niagara Falls.

That's not to say that a serious attempt wasn't made to retain at least one of the vessels. *Cayuga* had entered service in 1907 and continued her run to and from the Niagara River ports for a total of forty-four years. Citing various reasons, including the need for expensive safety upgrades brought on by the tragic fire that destroyed the upper lakes steamer SS *Noronic* here in Toronto Harbour in the fall of 1949, her owner, Canada

Toronto's skyline circa 1950. The tall office building is the Bank of Commerce (now Commerce Court North) on King Street just west of Yonge. Also visible is the Royal York Hotel before its 1959 addition. North and west of it is the stately Canada Life Building on University Avenue without its landmark weather beacon. In the middle of the view is the diminutive but dignified Toronto Harbour Commission Building and behind it the Postal Delivery Building, the south and east facades of which form part of today's Air Canada Centre. Moored at the Toronto Ferry Docks is the 1910 *Trillium* (restored in 1975) and to the extreme right is SS *Cayuga*, arguably the most popular of the Port of Toronto's several Lake Ontario passenger steamers.

The Great Lakes passenger steamer SS *Cayuga* as the popular vessel appeared on a circa-1920 souvenir postcard.

Steamship Line, quietly announced that *Cayuga* would not operate in 1952 and would be offered for sale or simply scrapped.

But enough people thought that *Cayuga* should continue to operate, which eventually resulted in the vessel being purchased, refitted, and returned to cross-lake service in time for the 1954 season. But it just wasn't to be. In 1957, the new company announced that it was all over. *Cayuga* was tied up alongside the dock wall near where Harbourfront Centre is located today and was slowly, methodically cut into little pieces. Lake Ontario passenger boat travel had truly come to an end.

# They Lined Up to Cross Niagara

## June 10, 2012

If all goes as planned, next Friday all eyes will be on, or should I say above, the Canadian Horseshoe Falls as daredevil Nik Wallenda performs his spectacular tightrope walk (an activity also known as funambulism) from Goat Island on the American side to Table Rock on our side. This will be the first time this particular route across the river has been attempted.

Historically, crossing the Niagara River was first attempted by French showman Jean Francois Gravelet, who performed as The Great Blondin more than a century and a half ago. But that event, and the dozens of similar tightrope crossings that followed, were all done across the river well north of the American and Horseshoe Falls and close to the whirlpool where the river bends and the gorge is approximately 275 metres wide.

Interestingly, among the many people who successfully crossed the river on a rope or wire were four young men from Ontario. The first was Port Hope's William Leonard Hunt, who as Signor Farini performed the feat in early September 1860. Exactly thirty years later, on September 6, 1890, Sam Dixon, one of our city's pioneer photographers and a frequent wire walker at the Hanlan's Point Amusement Park on Toronto Islands, became the first Torontonian to repeat Farini's exploit. He told the newspaper reporters covering the event that his crossing would be the first of many he planned to make over the next few years. Unfortunately, Dixon drowned the following year while swimming in Wood Lake near Bracebridge in Muskoka.

Another year passed, and on October 22, 1892, twenty-two-year-old Clifford Caverley became the second Torontonian to cross the gorge. Described in the newspapers of the day as "unmarried and weighing a mere 138 lbs," Caverley made several walks that day, one of which he accomplished in a record-setting 6 minutes, 32.5 seconds.

The third in the trio of Toronto funambulists was James Hardy, who had also perfected his talents at Hanlan's Point. He performed his Niagara River crossing on Dominion Day, 1896. He went on to cross the Montmorency Falls in Quebec a total of seventy-four times before travelling to England, where he performed wire walking performances in front of cheering crowds.

Hardy died of a heart attack at the age of sixty-four while shopping in a Queen Street West store. In his obituary that appeared in a Toronto newspaper, he was quoted as having once said, "when your time comes you'll get it whether you are 50 feet in the air or supposedly safe on the ground."

Both Hardy and Dixon are at rest in Mount Pleasant Cemetery.

Torontonian Samuel Dixon is shown in this rare photograph crossing the Niagara River on September 6, 1890, at a location not far from the Whirlpool Rapids. He drowned in a Muskoka lake the following year. The bridge in the photo is the old Michigan Central Railway cantilever bridge that was built in 1883 and replaced in 1925 by the present Michigan Central steel arch railway bridge. Two other Toronto boys, Clifford Caverley and James Hardy, crossed the river at this same location in 1892 and 1896, respectively.

# *Where Is Our Spitfire?*

## June 24, 2012

Several weeks ago I had a note from a reader asking if I had any recollection of a Second World War fighter aircraft that was on display somewhere close to Ontario Place. He seemed to recall that it was located near HMCS *Haida*, the iconic Canadian warship that had been given a home along the Ontario Place waterfront back in 1970 after five years moored at the foot of York Street.

And, his note went on, not far away there was another artifact from the Second World War, an Avro Lancaster bomber that had sat, rather forlornly, perched atop a concrete pedestal since the mid-1960s.

Having joined the staff of the CNE in 1974, I was familiar with the small collection that had accumulated just across Lake Shore Boulevard, a collection that, to some people, was starting to look like a museum dedicated to the Second World War. And perhaps that was the problem. War is not something certain people wish to celebrate, even though it brought the lifestyle we now treasure.

But back to the gentleman's original question: the fighter in question was, in fact, one of the more than twenty thousand Spitfires produced between 1936 and 1947. The "Spit" was a favourite of many RCAF pilots.

The Internet advises that the model on display on the Toronto waterfront was a rare Mark XIX variant (designated numerically as PM627), of which only 225 were produced. It served with the Royal Air

This Second World War Supermarine Spitfire was on display next to HMCS *Haida* at Ontario Place from 1972 to 1973. (Photo courtesy Richard E. Dumigan.)

The same aircraft is now a feature attraction in an aviation museum in Malmslatt, Sweden.

Force from 1945 to 1951, then with the Indian Air Force from 1953 to 1957, after which it was displayed in a museum in New Delhi.

In 1971, the aircraft was purchased by a member of the Canadian Fighter Pilots Association and shipped to Toronto, where it was put on display at the recently opened Ontario Place. There it sat from 1972 until 1973, when it was relocated to the Ontario Science Centre, where it remained until 1980. It then spent a couple of years in California before becoming part of a complicated trade that had "our" Spitfire sent to an aviation museum in Sweden in exchange for five (!!) other vintage aircraft.

As for the Malton, Ontario–built Lancaster (designated FM104) it was taken down from its pedestal in 1999 and transferred to the Canadian Air and Space Museum at Downsview. The future of this artifact, and the museum itself are, pardon the expression, up in the air.

In 2003, HMCS *Haida*, now a National Historic Site, began welcoming appreciative visitors at its new and friendlier home located at Pier 9 in Hamilton Harbour.

# Makin' Tracks Through History

## July 15, 2012

I'm pretty sure that by now anyone who drives the streets throughout downtown Toronto is aware of the ongoing closure of the busy Queen and Spadina intersection. And those TTC passengers who ride the 501 Queen streetcar will be given a special treat each day for the next week or so as they discover other parts of the downtown core as their vehicle manoeuvres around the closed intersection. It's all part of a major improvement program to upgrade sections of the Spadina streetcar right-of-way prior to the introduction of the TTC's new Legacy model vehicles later this year. Similar improvements and modifications to other parts of the system to accommodate the new Legacy cars are to come.

The history of street railway service on Spadina goes back more than 130 years to the day in 1878 when horse-drawn streetcars operated by the privately owned Toronto Railway Company (TRC) began carrying packed passenger cars over steel rails that had recently been laid on the stretch of Spadina Avenue between King and the fast-growing community around the Spadina and College intersection.

The city continued to expand northward, and in 1883 the Spadina route was extended all the way north to Bloor Street in order to serve what had only a few years earlier been rural countryside.

Then, in 1891, the Spadina line was incorporated into what the TRC had established as the Belt Line, a route that ran horse cars both ways on

Looking north on Spadina Avenue over Queen Street in 1924. Note the streetcars-only right-of-way down the centre of Spadina. The building on the northwest corner of the intersection was the site of one of the city's first silent movie houses. It was called the Mary Pickford Theatre in honour of the world-famous Toronto-born movie star. The present building houses a McDonald's restaurant.

Road and streetcar track repairs all up and down Spadina Avenue are nothing new. These men are hard at work in the summer of 1902, and note, doing it without today's mandatory safety equipment. In the distant background is Knox College, thankfully still a city landmark. The streetcars are operating on the popular Belt Line route.
(Both photos City of Toronto Archives.)

Bloor, Sherbourne, King, and Spadina, forming a "belt" around the city. On December 15 of the following year, the horse cars operating on the Belt Line were removed and newfangled electric streetcars introduced. This was the city's fourth all-electric route.

In the summer of 1923, the new Toronto Transportation Commission, not quite into the second full year of its mandate, discontinued the Belt Line and introduced a new Spadina route on which it operated double-end electric streetcars, initially between Bloor and Front and then, after 1927, over a new bridge that carried traffic over the busy railway corridor that still exists. An interesting feature of the TTC's new Spadina streetcar line was the fact that it featured double-end streetcars and crossover tracks at either terminus, thus precluding the need for loops to change direction. A similar way of changing direction will be featured on the new Eglinton Crosstown, Sheppard East, Finch West, and Scarborough RT light rail routes, all of which are scheduled to open in or before 2021.

Streetcar service on Spadina came to an end (but, as it would turn out, only temporarily) in the fall of 1948 when a serious shortage of electricity throughout the province prompted the TTC to replace the Spadina streetcars with buses.

Then, in a rather strange turn of events (especially in light of the fact that the TTC had decided to eliminate all of Toronto's streetcars by 1980 before reconsidering and deciding instead to retain its streetcars), plans were announced in 1992 to convert the Spadina bus route back to streetcar operation. This new streetcar route began operating on July 17, 1997.

# This 1910 Idea Was a Real Lifesaver

## July 22, 2012

As we enjoy the warm (often hot) weather months, it's particularly sad to learn about the numerous drownings that occur in our lakes and rivers or closer to home in someone's peaceful and beckoning backyard swimming pool.

While it's a difficult subject to write about, the eradication of these more often than not preventable accidents has been a concern for decades. In fact, in his letter to the mayor of Toronto back in 1910, Robert John Fleming, the general manager of the privately owned Toronto Railway Company (predecessor to today's TTC), stated that in his opinion every boy and girl should learn to swim. And to back up his conviction, Fleming declared that his company was prepared "to place at the disposal of the boys and girls of the city on every afternoon [except Sunday — not much was legal on Sunday back then] during the summer school holidays all of the special streetcars on different routes that will be necessary to transport to and from the respective free swimming stations throughout the city." And the company would do it without charge!

Fleming's only condition was that City Council must "provide at each swimming station a sufficient number of instructors and assistants for the purposes of properly caring for the children's lives and furthering the object of the service."

# CHILDREN
## LEARN TO SWIM

.............................

Supervised Swimming Stations are maintained by the City at **SUNNYSIDE, WESTERN SAND BAR, FISHERMAN'S ISLAND,** and on the **DON,** above Winchester Street.

Street Cars are provided daily by the Toronto Railway Company to carry children to these stations.

## ALL FREE OF CHARGE
.............................

### TIME-TABLE OF FREE STREET CARS

### To Sunnyside Swimming Station

Cars leave **KEELE AND DUNDAS STS. AT 1.00 P.M.,** via Dundas and Roncesvalles. Returning, leave Sunnyside at 4 p.m.

Cars leave **ROYCE AND LANSDOWNE AVES. AT 1.00 P.M.,** via Lansdowne, Dundas and Queen. Returning, leave Sunnyside at 4 p.m.

Cars leave **VAN HORNE AND DOVERCOURT AT 1.00 P.M.,** via Dovercourt Road and Queen. Returning, leave Sunnyside at 4 p.m.

### To Don Swimming Station

Cars leave **C.P.R. AND YONGE ST. AT 1.00 P.M.,** via Yonge, Carlton, Gerrard and Broadview to Danforth. Returning, leave Danforth at 4 p.m.

Cars leave **GERRARD AND GREENWOOD AT 1.30 P.M.,** via Gerrard and Broadview to Danforth. Returning, leave Danforth at 4.15 p.m.

### To Fisherman's Island Station

Cars leave **KINGSTON RD. AND QUEEN AT 1.30 P.M.,** via Queen, King, Church and Front to Yonge St. Returning, leave Yonge and Front at 4.05 p.m.

### To Western Sandbar Station

Cars leave **CHRISTIE AND DUPONT AT 1 P.M. AND 2.30 P.M.,** via Dupont and Bathurst to Front St. Returning, leave Front and Bathurst at 3 p.m. and 4.45 p.m.

### BOATS CONNECT WITH CAR SERVICES
.............................

## THE TORONTO RAILWAY CO.

In the summer of 1916, Toronto newspapers featured a series of ads like this one that listed details on how to take advantage of the Toronto Railway Company's "free bathing car" service.

It took some time to get the plan up and running, but eventually a summertime "free bathing car" service was in operation.

Three of the bathing stations where instructors hired by the city's Department of Public Health would teach children (who had arrived and would return home on the free streetcars) to swim were located at Sunnyside Beach (where years later the famous amusement park would open), on the Don River not far from the old Riverdale Zoo, and on the Western Sandbar (located across the old channel at the foot of Bathurst Street; the sandbar would eventually give way to Hanlan's Point and a new Island Airport).

A bobby-helmeted Toronto police officer assists two young Torontonians on board one of the city's "free bathing" streetcars after an afternoon of swimming lessons at Sunnyside on the western waterfront, circa 1925. Note the TTC inspector helping to keep some sort of order.

One additional bathing station was located on Fisherman's Island (now covered by the southernmost part of what is known as The Portlands). In addition to the free streetcar ride, getting to and from this facility required a ferryboat ride from the docks just south of the Yonge and Front intersection. The boat was provided, also free of charge, by Lawrence "Lol" Solman, the general manager of the Toronto Ferry Company, the same company that built the restored steam-powered *Trillium* that still paddles around Toronto Bay.

# Pleasant Streetcar History

## July 29, 2012

A couple of weeks ago I wrote about the evolution of the 510 Spadina streetcar line, which has become one of the city's busiest routes and one that traces its origins back to 1878. In anticipation of the arrival of Bombardier's state-of-the-art Legacy model streetcar, this route is presently undergoing major upgrading with its reopening scheduled for mid-November of this year.

That story prompted a reader living in North Toronto to ask if I could provide some details about the streetcar she recalled taking from her house near the corner of Eglinton and Mount Pleasant to the new Yonge subway; from there she travelled downtown to Eaton's main store. Known in its later days as the Mount Pleasant streetcar, like the Spadina route the line's origins go back almost a century (heck, it will be exactly a century next year) when the city established a street railway service along St. Clair Avenue. That line opened on August 25, 1913, and initially operated between Yonge Street and Station Street (now Caledonia Road). It was a unique service, since at the time almost all the other streetcar lines in the city were privately owned. The St. Clair route was part of the new Civic Railway system that was set up by the City of Toronto when it was unable (even after going to the highest courts in England) to get the private company that operated almost all of the local streetcar routes to improve and expand their

After more than half a century the presence of streetcars on Mount Pleasant Road came to a sudden end on July 24, 1976. Here one of the TTC's famed PCC vehicles on its way to the loop at Eglinton Avenue waits patiently at the Merton Street intersection. The Dominion Coal and Wood silos were neighbourhood landmarks for more than seven decades until being unceremoniously flattened in 2001.

operations to satisfy the needs of the fast growing municipality. This untenable situation began to be corrected in the fall of 1921 when the new municipally controlled TTC came into being and eventually took over all of the privately owned systems.

One of the routes to come under the TTC's umbrella was the St. Clair Civic Railway line. Interestingly, in its earliest form it operated on an exclusive centre of the street right-of-way, something that was removed between 1928 and 1935 (partly as one of many Depression make-work projects). History repeated itself when a new dedicated right-of-way was reinstated a couple of years ago. The eastern terminus of that early St. Clair route remained at Yonge Street until 1924, when track was laid on a new bridge built over the Vale of Avoca and then extended to a loop at Mount Pleasant Road, thereby serving the emerging Moore Park community. On August 15 of the following year, work began on extending track north on Mount Pleasant Road to a new loop laid out near the northeast corner of Eglinton Avenue.

In 1915, the City of Toronto paid the Toronto General Burying Grounds, trustees of Mount Pleasant Cemetery, nearly $100,000 to allow it to construct a roadway through the centre of the cemetery's property. Originally a farm, the property stretched from Yonge Street to the First Concession East (Bayview Avenue) and had been purchased by the trustees forty years earlier. When that new road was finally opened through the cemetery in the early 1920s, wet weather often made it impassable.

Streetcars were a familiar sight on Mount Pleasant Road from November 3, 1925, the day the line opened, until the plug was pulled (figuratively and literally) fifty years later following the Municipality of Metro Toronto's decision to rebuild the old bridge (opened in 1920 at a cost of $45,489) over the long abandoned Belt Line steam railway right-of-way south of Merton Street. Officials announced that streetcars were to be temporarily removed (or so the community was told) to allow work crews to build what was described as "a better bridge." The streetcars ran as normal on July 24, 1976, few realizing that after that day they would never return. And many said that it just wasn't the same when buses (electric trolley coaches, diesel powered, and hybrids) replaced them.

# From Civic to Simcoe

## August 5, 2012

The idea of a public holiday on the first Monday in August can be traced back to a proposal put forward by a few members of Toronto City Council in the late 1860s. It was their belief that citizens would appreciate a nice long weekend during those hot summers when air conditioning consisted of blowing across a large cake of ice, and that August would be the perfect time for it. However, it wouldn't be until 1875 that the necessary arrangements were finalized, and even then more than a few of the city's store and business owners were upset that their employees were getting a day off work (without pay).

Since no one really knew what to call this new holiday, it appears that it was simply given the rather nondescript title Civic Holiday.

(By the way, that inaugural date of 1875 confirms the fact that the holiday was not named in honour of a popular Japanese car, since the first Honda Civic didn't make its appearance for another ninety-eight years.)

The Civic Holiday title remained in effect for nearly a century until the provincial Minister of Tourism, James Auld, suggested in 1968 that the name be changed to honour the province's first lieutenant governor, John Graves Simcoe (the original David Onley). Auld's reasoning was that he could work this fellow Simcoe into his tourism mandate, while the term "Civic" had virtually no marketing potential aside from, as some believed, promoting a car.

John Graves Simcoe (1752–1806), the man for whom the holiday on the first Monday in August is named, unless you live outside Toronto that is. (Photo from the Ontario Archives.)

Toronto's Union Station was officially opened August 6, 1927, by Edward, the Prince of Wales. This wonderful photo of the station was taken in 1938, a date confirmed by fellow Thornhill Cruisers Car Club members Roger Ritter and Gary Lynas, two experts on identifying old cars. The streetcar is a large Peter Witt hauling a trailer, something I figured out by myself.

For whatever reason, Auld's suggestion went over like the proverbial lead balloon with most of the province's municipal officials. All except for Toronto's Mayor William Dennison, that is. His Worship managed to convince his council that this fellow Simcoe was more worthy of recognition than simply calling the day the Civic Holiday. As a result, a decree went out from City Hall affirming the fact that effective August 4, 1969, the first Monday in August would henceforth be known as Simcoe Day.

In addition to being the first lieutenant governor of Ontario (which was known back then as Upper Canada), Simcoe's most important Toronto connection was the fact that it was he who in 1793 ordered the establishment of a community that would evolve into the modern metropolis of which we are (or should be) proud in spite of her flaws.

Simcoe's plan for York (as he called the place after Frederick, Duke of York) was to make it the site of a well-protected naval shipyard where armed vessels that would help protect the young and vulnerable province against the military aspirations of our friends to the south would be built.

While Simcoe was to leave his Town of York in 1796 to carry out important responsibilities in other parts of the British Empire, his concerns about the invasion of our young province came to pass in 1812. This fascinating story will be featured at this year's CNE.

One other misconception about Simcoe's impact on our province is that he named Lake Simcoe after himself. Rather, it is in honour of his father, John (sometimes referred to as James) Simcoe, who served many years in the Royal Navy until succumbing to pneumonia on board his ship, HMS *Pembroke*, on May 15, 1759. Not only did Simcoe Sr. teach the explorer James Cook (Cook's Bay) the fundamentals of navigating and surveying, he is also said to have been responsible, in great measure, for the plans followed by James Wolfe that resulted in the invasion and capture of Quebec City in the fall of 1759.

# This Canuck Was a Golf God

## August 12, 2012

When the young ladies from Canada won the bronze medal for soccer last Thursday, they accomplished something that hadn't been done since 1904. It was 108 years ago, during the games held in St. Louis, Missouri, that the men's soccer team from Galt, Ontario (since 1973, Galt, Preston, and Hespeler have been part of the newly created City of Cambridge) won a medal in soccer, defeating the team from the United States — a stunning victory that resulted in a gold medal. That year saw Canadians win a total of six Olympic medals: four gold along with one silver and one bronze.

Interestingly, the other three of the four gold medals won by Canadians in 1904 were for the 56-pound throw, lacrosse, and golf) — none of which continue to be recognized as Olympic sports. For the record, the successful Canadian medal winners were, respectively, Montreal police officer Etienne Desmarteau, the Shamrock Lacrosse Team from Winnipeg, and from right here in Toronto our very own George Lyon. Seems as if every time a Canadian won a medal back then someone decided to remove the corresponding event from the list of eligible Olympic sports. And that Norwegian referee hadn't even been born yet.

But I digress … George Seymour Lyon was born in Richmond, Ontario (now, albeit reluctantly, part of the City of Ottawa) in 1858. As a young man he moved to Toronto and entered the life insurance business, eventually opening his own investment firm. George was an outstanding athlete in just about anything he tried his hand (or feet) at. He was especially skilled at cricket and track and field.

One day on the way home from a cricket match, George, now thirty-eight years of age, stopped by the Rosedale Golf Club (which was still located in the north end of the prestigious Rosedale neighbourhood) to watch a friend swinging away at a golf ball, something George had never even attempted. The friend persuaded George to give it a try, and after just a few swings George was hooked. In fact, he became so good at the game that over the next sixteen years the once reluctant golfer had won the Canadian amateur golf title a total of eight times. He accumulated many other titles as well and was soon identified as Canada's premier golfer.

On September 14, 1904, it was announced that the "tournament for the golf championship of the world" would be held as part of the Games of the III Olympiad and that the event would be held September 19–24 at St. Louis, Missouri's Glen Echo Country Club. Appended to the announcement were the names of more than fifty participants, including three players from Toronto's newly established Lambton Golf and Country Club. They were brothers A.E. and Bertie Austin and club captain George S. Lyon.

The concluding match of the tournament was held on September 24 and featured our George going up against American champion Chandler Egan. When the dust had settled Lyon was declared the greatest golfer in the world and awarded the gold medal.

Four years later Lyon had the opportunity of defending his title at the 1908 Olympics in London, England. However, when it was determined that no one was ready to challenge him, golf was abruptly removed from the list of Olympic events. Golf hasn't been part of the Summer Olympics since. However, it's being reinstated for the Rio de Janeiro games in 2016. And guess what, Toronto's George Lyon will remain as the Olympic gold medal title holder.

Unfortunately, he won't be there. George died in 1938 and now rests under one of the greens in our beautiful Mount Pleasant Cemetery.

Torontonian George Lyon was the last person to win the Olympic gold medal for golf. The year was 1904, and since it was never played at the Olympics again, George remains undefeated.

George Lyon died on May 11, 1938, at his Toronto residence on Garfield Avenue. Several years ago his monument in Mount Pleasant Cemetery was badly damaged, but thanks to some anonymous "fan" has since been nicely restored.

# Toronto Still Yonge at Heart

## August 19, 2012

Motorists who dare to use the lower portion of Yonge Street between Richmond and Gerrard over the next few weeks will come across a number of traffic restrictions that, it is hoped, will encourage greater pedestrian use and appreciation of what many regard as "Canada's Main Street." The Celebrate Yonge festival will continue until September 16.

Historically, most of the Richmond to Gerrard stretch of today's modern Yonge Street was a latecomer in the evolution of the thoroughfare that some still mistakenly describe as the longest street in the world. In fact, this one-time Guinness World Record holder was recently replaced when the title was given to the 29,800-mile-long Pan-American Highway, which is described as "the world's longest motorable road."

But I digress.… The idea of creating a Yonge Street originated soon after John Simcoe was appointed the first lieutenant governor of the newly established Province of Upper Canada (after 1867 renamed Ontario) back in 1791. Concerned about the vulnerability of his new province, he proposed that a military trail be constructed by his Queen's Rangers. This road (it was hardly that, more of a pathway) would serve as a relatively quick route to be taken by British troops stationed in forts located along the upper lakes to come the defence of the communities scattered along the southern border of the young province if and when troops from south

Yonge Street looking north over Queen Street, 1941. The numerous American flags on the old Eaton's store would indicate a special welcome to visitors from south of the border. Note also that right turns were permitted at this busy corner, as was parking on Yonge Street north of Queen. The Peter Witt "trains" would be replaced by the country's first subway in 1954.

of that border decided it was time to invade the province. (Actually, in Simcoe's mind it wasn't if an attack would come, but rather when.)

To this end, Simcoe's Rangers were ordered to cut a path through the forest and dense brush north of York, the site he had selected on the north shore of Lake Ontario to be the site of a naval shipyard. The plan was to have this pathway connect with watercourses not far from today's Holland Landing. Then, by using navigable lakes and rivers and Simcoe's new road, troops and weapons could get from the north down to the scene of any trouble with relative speed.

While that helps explain one of the reasons Yonge Street was laid out the way it was (another was its importance as a trading route for furs and other necessities), the road didn't originally penetrate into the downtown part of the city that we know today and incorporate the stretch that's part of the ongoing Celebrate Yonge festival. In fact, for many years swamps

Sir George Yonge (1731–1812) was a colleague of John Graves Simcoe before the latter was appointed our province's first lieutenant governor. Yonge was serving as the Secretary for War in King George III's cabinet when Simcoe honoured him with the name of what would become his new community's main street.

and other hindrances to the south of the Second Concession (now Bloor Street) forced travellers to veer east of the projected line of Yonge and enter the young community closer to its main business area near the King and Church street intersection. The name given to Toronto Street demonstrates that fact.

When the section south of Bloor was finally opened up there was another problem. South of today's Yonge and Queen intersection, the rambling tannery yard of pioneer industrialist Jesse Ketchum straddled Yonge Street's future right-of-way. Many more years would pass before Yonge Street would make its way to the water's edge.

# The Ill-Fated Ex of 1974

## August 26, 2012

When Exhibition time comes around each year, those of us who grew up in or near the city will no doubt reflect on the numerous childhood memories of our visits to the fair each summer. So what if the arrival of the Exhibition meant that going back to school wasn't far off? At least we'd have some book covers to wrap around the speller and some pencils to draw cars and airplanes in the margins. And with any luck maybe we'd be handed a wooden ruler with inches marked on it and a narrow steel edge to make straight lines in our five-cent Hilroy scribblers (Hilroy was actually Roy Hill, a Torontonian who started the company even before I was a kid). For sure all that free stuff would certainly help get us through the next ten months.

While I have fond memories of going to the Ex on the old Bathurst streetcar with my brother, mother, and aunt Peggy (dad and Uncle Ken weren't, I'm sorry to say, big fans of the fair … something about having to work for a living), my most vivid memories are reserved for those five years I was one of the devoted group of people that puts together the annual fair. In spite of my education in the field of chemistry, the fair's then general manager Dave Garrick was pretty sure that my love of Toronto history would be helpful in getting things ready for the CNE's Centennial Exhibition in 1978.

When I joined the staff several months before the start of the 1974 CNE I was given a few responsibilities to get my feet wet. After what happened that first year I began to wonder whether Dave was having second thoughts about what I had brought with me from my time with the Ontario Water Resources Commission (now the Ministry of the Environment).

My memories of the 1974 edition of the CNE are these: first, there was no TTC service whatsoever during the fair's run of twenty days. It would become the longest strike in TTC history. Through the media the general manager suggested people wanting to go to the Ex anyway should cross their arms in the shape of an "X" hoping that drivers headed that way would give them a lift. It worked. Attendance was only 13 percent off 1973 figures.

Then, one afternoon I was asked to retrieve motorcycle daredevil Evel Knievel's wife from the Royal York Hotel where they were staying awaiting the daredevil's performance. He was to attempt to jump thirteen large Mack trucks lined up side by side in front of the old Grandstand.

Needless to say, with the transit strike in full force the drive along Front Street to the hotel and back was, shall I say, a challenge, a challenge that soon got the better of me when at the Front and Spadina intersection my car's radiator let go and I was forced to retreat to the Esso station that used to be on the northeast corner. Suddenly, the aforementioned Mrs. Knievel exited the car and when last seen was walking north on Spadina headed for I know not where. When I phoned the office and tried to explain the situation to her husband his words back to me were few and totally unprintable in this family newspaper. Suffice it to say that my good wishes for a successful jump over those thirteen trucks were badly compromised.

And to top it off, when the fair was about to enter its second week, one of the CNE's largest exhibit buildings was destroyed by a fire that broke out late in the evening of August 23. Built in 1909 directly south of the Dufferin gate, it served for many years as the CNE's Transportation Building, where cars, trucks, and airplanes were on display before an amazed public. Later it was the Dance Pavilion (featuring Guy Lombardo and Rudy Vallée and the like) and eventually home to the most modern adding machines, typewriters, and other fascinating business products. I can hear the guy now: "Go ahead kids, give them a try, just don't break them or your dad'll have to pay the repair bill."

For 1974 it served as home to our feature country, Spain. For a time, anyway. The old building was full of artifacts, souvenir items, photos, murals, costumes, musical scores, and the like, all of which were lost in the conflagration.

What baggage had I brought to the Ex? Only time would tell. Suffice it to say they kept me around for another five years, then it was off to Canada's Wonderland.

This photo was taken soon after the CNE's new Ontario Government Building (left of view, now the Liberty Grand) opened to the crowds attending the 1926 Exhibition. In the background is one of the towers of the 1912 British Governments Building (later Arts, Crafts and Hobbies, now Medieval Times). The large structure to the right of the photo was completed in 1909. During my first year on staff at the CNE it was the site of the Spanish Pavilion. But not for long. A little over a week into the fair the old building was destroyed by fire.

# CNE's Back to the Future

## September 2, 2012

During its earliest years, what we now know as the Canadian National Exhibition (or simply the CNE or, even easier, the Ex) was the place to see the latest inventions. It didn't matter whether those new creations were for the farm (after all, the Ex had its genesis in the early 1800s as an agricultural fair), for industry (from 1879 until 1912 it was known as the Toronto Industrial Exhibition), or for the Canadian public, the CNE was looked upon as the showplace of the nation.

Over the years things have changed. Now instead of a trip to the CNE to try out the latest iPhone, BlackBerry, blueberry, megapixel digital camera, or incredibly fast laptop, inspect new household appliances, or perhaps spend some time checking out all the newest cars, it's off to Best Buy, the Bay, or the local car dealer.

One thing that has remained constant down through the years has been the idea of introducing the latest mass transit vehicles to the general public at the CNE. In fact, if we go back to the 1880s, the Exhibition was the site of a world first in the field of transportation. It was at the fair held in the fall of 1885 that Belgian-American inventor Charles Van Depoele got together with Toronto's John J. Wright (an inventor in his own right), and together they developed the world's first electric railway that collected electricity from an overhead wire using a trolley pole and small wheel. The electricity was then fed to motors located under the floor of their steel-wheeled vehicle. Revolutionary at the time, this particular current collecting feature was unique and continues to be used on all of the TTC's surface streetcars.

The experiment, though successful in 1885 with more than fifteen thousand amazed (and, more importantly, paying) passengers carried over the rails placed along the north side of the fairgrounds from a terminal near Strachan Avenue to a location near the present Music Building, had been less so during the Exhibitions held the previous two years. That was because the more common third rail form of power collection (such as that found in modern subways around the world) was used.

A spark of genius just prior to the 1885 fair (we're not sure whose spark it was, the Canadian's or the American's) prompted the idea of placing the power collection equipment up in the air, well away from the dangerous third rail and more importantly any wayward pedestrians.

The Exhibition's experimental railway continued for another few years. Its success led to the eventual electrification of the city's Church Street line in 1892. Within two more years all the previous horse car routes had been electrified. Passengers were happy … and I suppose so too were the horses.

Visitors to the 1885 edition of the Toronto Industrial Exhibition (the name wouldn't officially become the Canadian National Exhibition until 1912) were amazed to see and ride the newest public transit vehicle. And it was powered by the wonder of the age, electricity. Note the revolutionary trolley pole on the vehicle's roof.

Other displays related to improvements in public transit vehicles were featured at future Exhibitions. For instance, just as the TTC was about to come into being (exactly ninety-one years ago yesterday, happy anniversary, ladies and gentlemen) the latest in streetcar technology, widely known as the Peter Witt vehicle, was presented to the public attending the 1921 CNE.

Seventeen years later, fairgoers were wowed once again when two of the ultra-modern Presidents' Conference Committee (PCC) Streamliners were displayed at the 1938 CNE. The TTC went on to add a total of 743 PCCs (the majority new, along with some second-hand vehicles purchased from American transit companies) to its streetcar fleet. (Incidentally, two remain and can be chartered for special events.)

In 1978, number 4000, the first of the new Canadian Light Rail Vehicles (the model seen on today's city streets) was featured at the CNE's Centennial Exhibition. A prototype version had been featured at the fair in 1975. The larger, articulated version (ALRV) of this car was displayed at the 1982 edition of the Ex.

As the TTC gets ready to replace both the CLRV and ALRV vehicles in its fleet with new state-of-the-art equipment, mock-ups of possible replacement vehicles supplied by Bombardier and Siemens were featured at the 2007 CNE.

Now, as work gets underway on the construction of the first of the four new light rail lines, Metrolinx is featuring a mock-up of the LRT model scheduled for the Eglinton Crosstown line. It is located in front of the Direct Energy Centre.

The latest in a long list of public transit vehicles that have been displayed over the years at the annual CNE is a partial mock-up of the new Metrolinx light rail vehicle scheduled for use on (among others) the Eglinton Crosstown line. The mock-up is located in front of the Direct Energy Centre. This artist's rendition of a complete five-car train set was supplied courtesy Metrolinx.

# Stately Structures Indeed

## September 9, 2012

Located at the top of Toronto's University Avenue is the Ontario Legislative Building, a stately structure that is also known as the Parliament Buildings (to others it's known as the Pink Palace, and by a few as the Ontario gas works).

Now approaching 120 years of service, it is one of the most recognizable buildings in the province. However, as "ancient" as it may be, it is in fact only the latest in a long list of buildings of various shapes and sizes that have served the governments of the Province of Upper Canada, then the Province of Canada, and finally the Province of Ontario.

The first provincial parliament building was located in Navy Hall in Newark (now Niagara-on-the-Lake). The legislative assembly was subsequently relocated to the Town of York (now Toronto) to a site considered to be more secure than Navy Hall, a building that stood within canon shot of those threatening American troops across the Niagara River. As it turned out, the supposedly secure site at York wasn't. The structure was destroyed by fire during the American invasion of our community in April 1813. (More details about this site and the War of 1812 battles are revealed at the Ontario Heritage Foundation's First Parliament Building exhibition hall at the southeast corner of Front and Berkeley streets.)

Front Street looking east to Simcoe Street, circa 1953. The third Parliament Building was demolished in the early 1900s and replaced by the CPR freight sheds located in behind the Peter Witt streetcar on the Bathurst route. Note the Barclay (now demolished) and Royal York hotels in the background.

The third Provincial Parliament Buildings on the north side of Front west of Simcoe Street. (Photo from the Ontario Archives.)

As the years went by, successive legislative assemblies relocated into a variety of buildings. Finally, officials got their act together, and in 1832 a new building on the north side of Front Street just west of Simcoe was erected and became the third "real" parliament building.

When the Dominion of Canada, consisting of the provinces of New Brunswick, Nova Scotia, and the Province of Canada (Canada East and Canada West) came into being in 1867, the former Canada West, now renamed the Province of Ontario, became the sole occupant of the Front Street building.

The rundown old building endured for several more decades and was finally replaced by the fourth Ontario Legislative Building. Designed by English architect Richard Waite (the selection of the "foreigner's" design is a story all by itself) and built at a cost of $1.25 million, it opened for business at the top of University Avenue on April 4, 1893.

# World's First Movie Star

## September 16, 2012

During this year's Toronto International Film Festival there were (and perhaps still are) dozens of celebrities from the wonderful world of motion pictures visiting many of the numerous restaurants and theatres our fair city has to offer. Now, as the film fest winds down for another year and rave reviews proliferate, it's high time to take notice of the person who is universally accepted as being the very first of these motion picture celebrities. In fact, most experts regard this person as the first to be given the title "movie star." And what's more, this star was born right here in Toronto.

While this person would eventually become known to the world by the name Mary Pickford, to the few Torontonians of the 1890s who knew the youngster, she was just the little girl who lived in the small two-storey house at 175 University Avenue, an inconspicuous place on the edge of the infamous Ward part of town. To them, she was simply Gladys Smith.

Just how little Gladys went from playing on the dusty streets of Toronto to playing on playhouse stages across America and eventually onto silent movie theatre screens around the world as Mary Pickford, a stage name she herself chose from her family tree, are fascinating stories. However, suffice it to say that neither of these things would have happened, nor would we now be celebrating this famous Canadian, had it not been for her father's misfortune.

University Avenue looking north to College Street as the street looked about the time Gladys was born in a small house just out of view to the right.

John Charles Smith married a Toronto lass by the name of Charlotte Hennessey. Together they had three children, Lottie, Jack, and Gladys. The latter (the future Mary Pickford) was born on April 8, 1892. Sadly, her father descended into alcoholism, an all-too-frequent illness amongst the lower classes. This condition eventually led to serious medical problems and quite probably to John's death in the depths of the winter of 1898.

In Mary's memories she is a little more charitable, suggesting her father passed away after cracking open his skull while loading barrels onto one of the Lake Ontario passenger boats. With much of the lake frozen over, one has to question her suggestion that her father died on a passenger boat in the winter.

However it happened, the family's breadwinner was dead. A distraught mother quickly sought a way to look after her family. She was aware that even at the age of six, Gladys had shown a remarkable talent for acting. One of the rooms in the Smiths' University Avenue house was rented to a member of a stage company that was in town to perform *The Silver King* at the Princess Theatre on King Street West (demolished years later when the extension of University Avenue was pushed through to Front Street), and it was his idea to put the youngster's name forward as the person to fill a small part in the play. Perfect for the part, Gladys was hired. The payment was small, but her career in show business had gotten off to a good start.

Toronto's own Gladys Marie Smith, inset above, who would become better known to the world as Mary Pickford.

Gladys's 1892 birthplace on University Avenue. A portion of this site would later be occupied by the world-famous Hospital for Sick Children.

Those in the business convinced Gladys that she would have to change her rather undistinguished name to a more identifiable one. Gladys herself selected Mary Pickford, with the first name a variation on her own middle name, Marie. Her new surname would honour her favourite grandfather, John Pickford Hennessy.

Looking back, it was a strange twist of fate that resulted in Toronto's Gladys Smith becoming the world's first movie star, the lady they would call America's Sweetheart.

# Streamlining T.O.'s Streets

## September 23, 2012

When we look through the record books, today's date is an especially interesting one when it comes to transportation milestones in our city's history. The first event has to do with public transportation here in Toronto, the other with a form of transportation that helped the Allies win the Second World War. Got your attention, eh?

It was on this day back in 1938 that Torontonians, who for decades had relied on a variety of less-than-agreeable street railway vehicles, were finally introduced to the latest model streetcar, the amazing PCC Streamliner. I use the term *amazing* not without reason since up until now the seventeen-year-old Toronto Transit Commission's fleet of streetcars had been made up of Peter Witt motors and trailers (true, the best equipment available when the new TTC went into business) augmented with a collection of ancient wooden vehicles and a small selection of tired double-ended steel ones, all of which had been part of the city's previous transit operators' fleets. These latter cars had been part of the takeover arrangements when the private transportation companies were replaced by the new municipally controlled TTC in September 1921.

For sure, the TTC's customers (and city taxpayers) were getting restless. They were eager to see major improvements take place after so many years. And when they finally were able to ride the fast and comfortable new PCCs they were truly amazed.

This photo shows Mayor Ralph Day introducing Torontonians to the first of the state-of-the-art PCC Streamliner streetcars that entered service on the St. Clair line on September 23, 1938. (Photo from the TTC Archives.)

The first two of these new PCC vehicles had already been seen and admired by thousands attending the CNE earlier that summer. A few weeks went by, and after some last-minute kinks were worked out it was time to put the new PCCs into revenue service. The cars were assigned to the St. Clair route and stored in the carhouse on Wychwood Avenue that has since been cleverly converted into the Wychwood Barns.

Over the decades the PCC fleet grew to over seven hundred vehicles, most of them new plus more than two hundred second-hand vehicles purchased from American cities that had rejected the streetcar in favour of buses. Some of those cities are now returning to the streetcar as a "new" mode of transit.

It was in December 1995 that the last Toronto PCC streetcar operated in regular revenue service. Now only two remain, held onto for special service and events. Even as I write this column, the TTC is anticipating the arrival of the first of 204 LFLRVs (Low Floor, Light Rail Vehicles) one of the most modern street railway vehicles anywhere in the world! And just as Torontonians did in 1938, we'll welcome them. But the PCC won't soon be forgotten.

One of the TTC's ubiquitous PCC streetcars glides through the Dundas and Yonge intersection in this photo supplied by John Bromley. The Brown Derby ("All you can eat spaghetti, 99¢") was a landmark on this corner for years, as was the O'Keefe Brewery seen in the right background. The corner now features a plethora of gaudy neon signs.

I alluded to a second transportation-related event that occurred in, or, to be precise, near Toronto exactly eight years after the first of Toronto's new PCC streetcars entered service. It was on September 23, 1942, that the first of over a thousand Canadian-built Mosquito aircraft took to the air at the Downsview factory of de Havilland Aircraft of Canada (a company that had set up shop in Canada in 1927 and was purchased by Bombardier in the late 1980s). The Mosquito went on to become one of the most important aircraft of the Second World War. Oh, and just how is this event transportation-related? Among other Canadian-built aircraft, the Downsview Mosquitos helped "deliver" many of the knockout blows that helped bring the war to a successful end.

# Rollin', Rollin' Down the River

## September 30, 2012

Over the years I have devoted several columns to a remarkable, though not particularly successful, Canadian invention: the "roller boat" that was designed by Prescott, Ontario, lawyer Frederick Knapp. And while the story has been told and re-told, it's always great when an anniversary of a roller boat incident comes around, an anniversary that allows me to continue to tell the saga of Knapp's bizarre creation.

However, before I describe the September 28, 1907, event that prompted this column, let me briefly describe for those who are unfamiliar with the roller boat what Knapp had in mind when he came up with his unusual seafaring creation.

Knapp's idea was to build a vessel that would be impervious to the often serious effects of rough water and dangerous waves that made passengers seasick and often resulted in damaged freight. To achieve this characteristic, his vessel would utilize what he called the "inertia of motion." To prove his design would work, Knapp journeyed to Toronto and arranged for the Polson Iron Works (incidentally the same company that would build the Toronto Islands ferry *Trillium* a dozen years later) to build a prototype of his craft at the company shipyard at the foot of Sherbourne Street. Years of landfilling would place the yard today close to where the busy cross-waterfront railway corridor passes over Sherbourne Street.

Curiosity brought these people to Toronto's waterfront, where they discovered the long since abandoned roller boat.

The Toronto-Hamilton passenger steamer SS *Turbinia*, a victim of the unplanned voyage of Knapp's experimental craft on September 28, 1907.

Paying close attention to the inventor's plans, the craft that Polson finally came up with was something akin to a huge, hollow rolling pin more than 30 metres in length with an outside diameter of 6.5 metres. Passengers and/or freight would be carried inside the vessel in a kind of squirrel-cage affair that through the use of small wheels and tracks remained level as the outer shell, powered by small steam engines at either end, spun slowly at approximately six revolutions per minute. Long paddles affixed lengthwise to the outer shell propelled the craft through, or should I say over, the water.

Prescott, Ontario, lawyer, inventor, and dreamer Frederick Knapp.

Launched on September 9, 1897, the $60,000 experimental craft made its initial trip on Toronto Bay six weeks later. Spinning across the water, the craft made little headway that day, especially as it travelled lengthwise into strong lake winds that sprang up. In future test trips the revolutions were increased tenfold, but the change made little difference. Disappointed, but still convinced he was on to something, Knapp returned to the drawing board back in his Prescott residence (a house that I'm advised still stands).

What happened to the roller boat now becomes difficult to follow. We do know that the Polson company wanted the rest of its money, while Knapp demanded that his experimental craft be converted into a coal carrier so he could sell it to recoup at least some of his investment. More years went by, and still nothing happened. Until, that is, that stormy day in September 1907 when the roller boat broke loose from its moorings, floated west along the waterfront, and hit the passenger steamer SS *Turbinia*, berthed near the foot of Yonge Street. New litigation followed as the owners of *Turbinia* sued Knapp for damages amounting to $600, while Knapp sued the Polson company for $30,000 for letting his craft escape while it was supposedly under the company's care. For all I know, those cases are still in court.

More years passed. When we next read about the roller boat the year was 1925 and the steel hulk, now rusted and full of holes, was being hauled on shore ready to be buried in the mud and muck that was being added along the shoreline to create the new waterfront. Is the strange skeleton still there, under all those railway tracks?

Oh, and what happened to Fred Knapp? A friend told a Toronto newspaper that during the Great War Knapp had worked on plan for a super freighter based on his roller boat design. He tried to convince officials of the Royal Navy that a ship that rolled *over* the water would certainly avoid those "damned" German torpedoes.

# Keewatin *Comes Home*

## October 7, 2012

Back in June of this year my wife and I spent a wonderful few hours on board the tug *Prescotont* watching in amazement as the former Great Lakes passenger ship SS *Keewatin* made her way at the end of the tug *Wendy Anne*'s tow rope through the narrows at Giants Tomb Island, then across Georgian Bay and into the sheltered harbour at Port McNicoll.

Interestingly, the captain of the tug, who had the responsibility of returning the 102-metre-long vessel from Douglas, Michigan, where she had been a floating museum for nearly forty-five years, to Port McNicoll, the iconic passenger ship's home port from 1912 until 1965, was convinced that his charge was so eager to get home that she kept trying to pass his tug.

Upon the ship's arrival, the reception afforded SS *Keewatin* was overwhelming, with hundreds of local citizens, numerous first-time visitors to the region, a community band, and even an entertaining choir giving a nice welcome to the huge flotilla of pleasure boats, police craft, and even a helicopter that accompanied the homeward-bound SS *Keewatin*.

According to the ship's project manager Eric Conroy (aka Captain Rik), getting the vessel home was the easy part. He was pretty sure that getting her ready for the public would be a lot more difficult. However, once word got around that SS *Keewatin* was coming home, it wasn't long before a huge number of volunteers, from far and near, were eager to get the ship ready for her official public opening next spring. In fact,

SS *Keewatin*'s dining room is virtually intact.

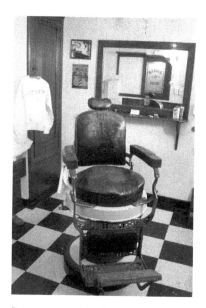

Passengers wishing for a shave and a haircut during their voyage could visit the ship's barbershop. All that's missing today is the barber.

enough has been accomplished thus far by many of those "*Keewatin*-ites" to permit members of the public to come aboard and see what's been accomplished thus far. Yarmila and I had that opportunity earlier this week. All we can say is "Wow!!"

By the way, SS *Keewatin* hopes to continue welcoming visitors as long as there's nice weather, perhaps even as late as Halloween. For more details about the ship, when it's open to the public, and how to find her location on Georgian Bay, check out the ship's website, sskeewatin.com.

In this rare photograph taken sometime in 1950, SS *Keewatin* departs the Port McNicoll dock bound for Port Arthur. Note the grain elevators in the background. Their presence and the numerous freighters that would utilize them made both the harbour and the town incredibly busy places. The landmark elevators were demolished a couple of years ago. (Photo from the Keewatin Collection.)

# Tunnel Comes in for Landing

## October 14, 2012

We often read about construction projects that go over budget and/or past scheduled completion dates. Some ventures miss by only a few dollars or a few months, while others miss by a year and perhaps millions of dollars. But there's one project here in Toronto that was actually started seventy-seven years ago and its completion is still a couple of years away.

Work on the Island Airport pedestrian tunnel that's now being built by the Toronto Port Authority under the Western Channel began earlier this year. Nearly 245 metres in length and almost 30 metres beneath the water, this $82.5-million tunnel will feature four moving sidewalks and will connect the Billy Bishop Toronto City Airport at Hanlan's Point with the mainland at the foot of Bathurst Street.

To suggest that the building of a tunnel under the Western Channel began seventy-seven years ago really needs some explaining. It was in the fall of 1935 that work began on building what was to be a $976,300 tunnel under the channel to connect the mainland with the Western Sandbar that after much land reclamation would become the site of Toronto's main airport.

This tunnel was to be 665 metres long, 16.5 metres wide, and incorporate streetcar tracks and two sidewalks. It would be constructed of reinforced concrete, be elliptical in shape, and rest almost twenty metres below the bottom of the channel.

In October 1935 construction began on a tunnel under the Western Channel that would connect the foot of Bathurst Street with what was being proposed as the city's main airport located at Hanlan's Point on Toronto Island. In the background is the now demolished Maple Leaf Mills grain elevator and (left) the Canada Malting elevator that's still there, but no longer in use.

The bulk of the money to complete the project had been promised by the federal Conservative government under Prime Minister R.B. Bennett, with the city contributing exactly $125,053.

As mentioned, when work started there was no airport at the south end of the tunnel. Nor would there be one for another three years. Interestingly, in anticipation of the 1939 visit to Canada by the reigning monarch and his wife (her first and King George VI's only visit), Toronto city officials chose Port George VI Island Airport as the new field's official title. Since then the name has changed several times: Toronto Island Airport, Toronto City Centre Airport, and the present Billy Bishop Toronto City Airport.

The saga of the original airport tunnel comes to an abrupt end on October 14, 1935, a little more than a week after construction began. It was on that day that a federal election resulted in the Conservative party being ousted by the Liberals under William Lyon Mackenzie King. The

For many years access to the airport on Toronto Islands was across the Western Channel via this converted barge. Note Toronto's famous International League baseball stadium (demolished in 1968) and the remnants of Little Norway (a military base, then wartime housing, and now the site of a city park) in the background of this 1955 photo.

new prime minister was not a big fan of Toronto and ordered that money promised for the airport tunnel be withdrawn.

When the airport opened in 1938, without that tunnel, the only access to and from was by a converted Montreal Harbour barge hauled across the channel by a winch and rope mechanism. That lasted until 1963, when the barge was replaced by a tug. It was eventually replaced by a succession of small ferries: *Maple City, Windmill Point*, and the present *Marilyn Bell* and *David Hornell*. I wonder what will happen with the last two when the tunnel finally opens?

# Mother Parker Turns One Hundred

## November 4, 2012

The year was 1912, and thirty-three-year-old Stafford Higgins, along with his wife, Belinda, had just moved to Toronto from Collingwood. It was here in the bustling city of nearly half a million citizens that Stafford and his business partner, William Burke, decided to go into the very competitive wholesale grocery business. With dozens and dozens of local grocery stores scattered across the city, getting their business up and running was a serious challenge. But it wasn't long before the new Higgins and Burke Ltd., now located at 33 Front Street, steps west of the busy St. Lawrence Market, began to flourish. Business continued to improve, and eventually Higgins was able to purchase Burke's interest in the growing enterprise.

Over the years the company's local business continued to grow, and thanks to Stafford Higgins's contacts throughout the mining and highway building camps located in the wilds of northern Ontario it was soon supplemented by extensive out-of-town sales. And while it's true that the Great Depression took its toll on most businesses, it's equally true that people still had to eat. As a result the grocery business, including that of the company that was still identified as Higgins and Burke, suffered less than most.

The next major venture for the company occurred soon after Stafford's second eldest son, Paul, joined the company. As the 1930s dawned the young man noticed that tea was quickly becoming the beverage of choice for many Torontonians. After extensive research the company developed its new product, giving it a name and a face thanks to the artistic talents of Stafford's wife, Belinda, and with sage advice from his good friend Frank O'Connor, whose Laura Secord chocolates had become a well known name (and face) in the city's numerous candy stores. It wasn't long before Mother Parker was "born."

In 1934, the same year that Toronto turned one hundred, Mother Parker's Tea began appearing on grocery store shelves. A couple of years later the company introduced a special roasted coffee. The success of these two products prompted the company to rename itself Mother Parker's Tea and Coffee Limited. Soon Mother Parker became a familiar face on hundreds of Canadian store shelves. Now, as this all-Canadian company celebrates its centennial year, the achievements of Mother Parker's Tea and Coffee Limited continue to be recognized worldwide.

Mother Parker's fleet of delivery trucks parked on lower Bay Street, 1939. Note the Toronto Harbour Commission Building to the extreme right of the view.

The legendary Mother Parker.

# Belt Line Was Short-Tracked

## November 18, 2012

One of the ongoing challenges (amongst many, I'm sure) facing those who run this city is to provide its citizens with safe, fast, affordable, and efficient public transportation. Whether people get there and back by streetcar (and eventually by light rail vehicles), bus, or subway, these modes of travel must continually be improved, upgraded, and integrated with other transit services in the surrounding communities.

Unfortunately, our track (pun intended) record when it comes to keeping ahead of the curve, especially when it comes to subway construction, is less than stellar. Take for instance the building of Toronto's (and Canada's) first subway. It took several decades just to get the idea approved and another five years to actually build the original section of the Yonge line (Union Station to Eglinton Avenue), with the less than five-mile-long line finally opening on March 30, 1954.

Another nine years went by before the city's subway mileage was increased with the opening of an extension to the Yonge line under University Avenue running north to a terminal at the new St. George station. Three years went by, and in 1966 the original stretch of the Bloor-Danforth subway (Keele and Woodbine) opened. In the years that followed a couple of extensions were added that resulted in the present Kipling on the west to Kennedy on the east configuration that in its present form will celebrate its thirty-second anniversary later this week.

After the Belt Line commuter railway failed in November 1894 the tracks were used by the Grand Trunk (later the Canadian National) Railway to move freight. After the tracks were removed the right-of-way became part of the City of Toronto's Belt Line Linear Park.

Not to be left out, the original Yonge subway continued to be lengthened, first from Eglinton to York Mills in 1973 and then on to Finch the next year. At the other end of this line what is now the Spadina part of today's Yonge-University-Spadina subway was added with the opening of the St. George to Wilson stretch in 1978. A full eighteen years passed before Yonge trains headed north over Highway 401 and into the new Downsview station. Plans initially called for this station to be the western terminal of a future Sheppard subway that would have as its eastern terminus the Scarborough Town Centre. That idea came off the rails (pun intended) and what we got was a Sheppard line that ran from Yonge Street to Don Mills Road. It opened (are you ready for this?) exactly ten years ago.

And yes, subway work continues with a further extension of the Yonge-University-Spadina subway into the City of Vaughan scheduled for completion four or five years from now.

Long before the TTC and GO Transit got into the public transportation business there was a much earlier attempt to provide a passenger service from downtown out into the city's hinterland. It would be provided

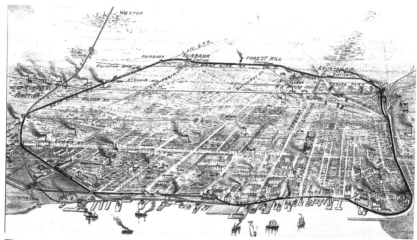

This map of the Belt Land Company's proposed commuter line appeared in a promotional brochure titled *The Highlands of Toronto*. The purpose of this intriguing steam railway venture was to promote the sale of land that the company held in the hinterlands outside the city limits.

by a new company call the Belt Land Corporation, which had acquired hundreds of acres of land well north of the city in and around the Third and Fourth Concession roads (today's St. Clair and Eglinton avenues). As an inducement to get Torontonians to purchase this land, the company promised to provide easy access to and from the purchaser's nice quiet home in the suburbs and his work in the bustling downtown core using steam locomotives hauling passenger cars over tracks that encircled the young city.

The first Belt Line train ran on July 30, 1892. Things went relatively smoothly until the price to ride the Belt Line in combination with a worldwide mini-depression and the resulting drop in housing and land sales forced officials of the Belt Land Company to curtail railway operations on November 17, 1894 (exactly 118 years ago yesterday). In total this interesting public transit venture lasted a mere 840 days.

Over the following years trains used the former Belt Line tracks as a freight line that served several small companies that were established along the right-of-way. Today, this same right-of-way has been incorporated into the Belt Line Linear Park that was championed by Mayor David Crombie and local city politician Kay Gardner.

# Wharf Lighthouse Turns 150

## November 25, 2012

When we talk about preserving our city's history we usually talk about saving old buildings. Prominent structures such as Mackenzie House on Bond Street (home of Toronto's first mayor), Campbell House (built in 1822, relocated in 1972 to the northwest corner of University and Queen from Duke Street, now Adelaide Street East) in the old Town of York, the 1892 Gooderham (Flatiron) Building

The Queen's Wharf lighthouse (seen in this view behind the Harbourmaster's residence) was erected in 1861 as a navigational aid to assist ships entering Toronto Harbour through the old and frequently dangerous Western Channel. That channel was located some distance north of the present West Gap on a site that approximates today's busy Lake Shore Boulevard and Bathurst Street intersection.

at the Front, Wellington, and Church intersection, or our beloved Old City Hall (1899) come to mind. Less obvious but no less historically important is the Queen's Wharf lighthouse on the north side of Lake Shore Boulevard just west of Bathurst Street. Thousands of cars and trucks whiz by it every day (except during rush hour, when they stagger by) while inside each cozy vehicle drivers and passengers alike pay little or no attention to this important structure that has just celebrated, without any fanfare, its 150th anniversary. The lighthouse's sesquicentennial story is briefly told in the three photos that accompany this column.

Years went by, and it wasn't until early in 1929 that the Toronto Harbour Commission (now the Toronto Port Authority) agreed to preserve this long-abandoned reminder of the city's water-front history. Later that same year the lighthouse was moved west along The Boulevard (now Lake Shore Boulevard) to its present location with the aid of horses pulling it over a series of wooden rollers.

You know time is passing when your own photos become historic. I took this view when the lighthouse wore a coat of historically incorrect white paint, the once ubiquitous PCC vehicle was the most modern streetcar the TTC operated, and the Molson Brewery on the north side of Fleet Street east of Bathurst was still in full operation. Opened in 1955, the plant was closed almost a decade ago and subsequently demolished. Although modern condominiums now line the north side of Fleet Street and the TTC's newest streetcars use the aptly named Lighthouse Loop (which opened in 1931), the "ancient" lighthouse continues to remind us of Toronto's nautical past.

# The Very First Grey Cup

## December 2, 2012

Anyone who reads this week's "The Way We Were" article will say, "Why didn't you run this column last week? After all, that was Grey Cup Sunday." To be sure, I toyed with the idea, but decided that there would be so much in the media related to that special one hundredth Grey Cup game that the story I wanted to tell about the very first Grey Cup game would probably have been lost in all the hoopla. So, I saved it for this week. And it makes some sense, since it was 103 years ago this coming Tuesday that the very first of the annual contests for the newly minted Grey Cup was held. But wait a minute. If that very first game was held on December 4, 1909, how is it that last Sunday's game was the one hundredth? If it's an annual event then the calculation doesn't work. Turns out, like many other events in the tumultuous years of the Great War, the Grey Cup competition was cancelled in 1916, 1917, and 1918. So that accounts for three of the missing years, and as for the missing fourth year the teams that were to compete in 1919 each represented a different league. Unfortunately, each league had a different set of rules, and when the teams couldn't agree on which set to follow the resulting stand-off prompted the decision to forego the 1919 Grey Cup game altogether.

Now that the rather confusing numerical details are out of the way, let's look at some of the more interesting facts about the very first Grey Cup game that took place in front of 3,807 spectators on a field in the

fashionable Rosedale part of the city more than 100 years ago. The competitors for the trophy presented by the country's ninth governor general, one Albert Henry George Grey, the fourth Earl Grey (who was actually more of a hockey fan than a football fan, but a cup for that sport had been donated earlier in 1909 by Sir Montagu Allan), were teams representing the University of Toronto and the Parkdale Canoe Club (now the Boulevard Club). Now we know why the fellows on the latter club were known as "Parkdale Paddlers."

The game was 6–5 at halftime with the Varsity boys scoring five points for a "try" (touchdown) and a single point, or "rouge" (for the ball going out-of-bounds), while the Paddlers had one try. In the second half Varsity scored two tries, nine rouges, and a convert (a point after a touchdown), while the Paddlers could score only one rouge. The final score of the first Grey Cup game was 26–6 in favour of U of T.

Here's another interesting historical fact from the first Grey Cup game: the first six points (one try plus a rouge) were scored by Hugh Gall. Gall was born in Toronto and attended local public schools and Parkdale Collegiate. He graduated from U of T's School of Practical Science. During the Great War he served with the Canadian Engineers and saw service at Ypres, the Somme, and Cambrai. He was only forty-nine when he succumbed to pneumonia. Hugh Gall, one of this country's pioneer football stars, is buried in Mount Pleasant Cemetery.

The first Grey Cup game was played on Rosedale field on December 4, 1909, with the team from U of T easily defeating the Parkdale Paddlers. If that's the case, why was the one-hundredth Grey Cup game played in 2012? And why in the world was one of the teams called the Paddlers? Read on, dear reader.

Captain of the University of Toronto's football team Hugh Gall scored the first six points in that first ever Grey Cup game.

# Travels Back in Time

## December 16, 2012

In the days before GO buses and GO trains and multi-lane super-highways, country folk who planned on visiting Toronto, whether on business or just to see friends, faced an often arduous multi-day excursion. This was particularly true during the winter months when, as I've read, the roads were often impassable and the weather much worse than we have it these days with bone-chilling temperatures and snowstorms that would create drifts as high as a horse's withers.

One of numerous small hostelries on rural Yonge Street, the York Mills Hotel was a favourite gathering place for several bicycle clubs in the late 1800s and early 1900s.

With conditions such as these, it's easy to see why the small hotels and taverns scattered alongside the roads that led to and from the big city, such as the Dundas Highway, the Kingston Road, and Yonge Street, were so popular. While the vast majority of such roadside landmarks have vanished, one does remain today. And while the Miller Tavern, situated on the east side of Yonge Street just south of the busy Wilson–York Mills intersection (and for us old-timers to the north of the old city limits at Glen Echo and Yonge Boulevard), no longer provides overnight accommodation, guests continue to enjoy food and drink just as those cold and hungry visitors did a century and more ago.

The present Miller structure dates from the mid-1850s and was built by the Hogg brothers, John and William, to replace an earlier hotel on the site that had been destroyed by fire. Interestingly, the Hogg brothers have the distinction of being the developers of one the province's earliest subdivisions, creating a community that grew in and around Hogg's Hollow.

A few decades later the old hotel became the site of a different kind of recreational pastime. This sketch was used in the long-defunct *Evening Telegram* newspaper to illustrate an article that described a police raid in early January 1934.

Over the ensuing years the brothers' hotel would be known by several different names, the most prominent being the York Mills Hotel (named for the water-powered mills north of the Town of York). The hostelry quickly became known far and wide as Birrell's Hotel when David Birrell, assumed ownership. Still later the name was changed to the Jolly Miller Hotel, and many will remember summertime swims in the nearby pool or skating on the rink that would magically appear behind the hotel in the depths of those far-off winters. Overnight accommodation in the hotel ended in 1964.

One of the most interesting features of the Jolly Miller was its location outside the Toronto city police department's area of responsibility. And because the township and county police were few in number and had huge areas to patrol their officers were infrequently seen in or near the hotel. As a result the Jolly Miller became notorious for the gambling activities that took place within. The sketch that accompanies this column appeared in a January 8, 1934, *Evening Telegram* newspaper article that reported on a particularly aggressive raid on the place by Toronto and York Country police officers.

In 1997, the old building and the surrounding land was purchased by the municipality and a search was started for a new tenant. It took time, but eventually, after a multi-million-dollar restoration project, the old landmark, now simply known as the Miller Tavern, has once again assumed its place as a welcoming spot along the way.

# Gardiner in a Pickle

## December 23, 2012

Toronto's Frederick G. Gardiner Expressway — fix it up, tear it down, move it, bury it, sell it ... oh, what to do?

Originally described as either the Cross-Waterfront Highway or the Lakeshore Highway and even the Lakeshore Expressway, what is now called simply the Gardiner Expressway first appeared on the municipal election ballot cast on January 1 for the year 1948 (for many years municipal elections were held on New Year's Day). The question to be asked of Toronto voters read:

> Are you in favour of the City as the first stage of an express highway along the waterfront between the Humber River and the Don Valley Road the construction of a highway approximately parallel to the right-of-way of the Canadian National Railway between the east bank of the Humber River and Fleet Street [Lake Shore Boulevard] at Strachan Ave. as recommended by the City Planning Board at an estimated cost of $6.5 million?

That was what was supposed to happen. However, a serious shortage of steel for a variety of other projects (power plants, schools, hospitals, etc.) resulted in city officials deciding to remove the question from the

In this aerial view taken in the spring of 1961 by Les Baxter for the *Toronto Telegram* newspaper we see the Jameson Avenue to Spadina Avenue section of the new Gardiner Expressway under construction. This stretch opened in June of the following year. At the centre left of the photo we can see just how close the new highway came to impacting the southwest ramparts of historic Fort York.

ballot even though traffic congestion throughout the downtown core was becoming a problem, one that the experts predicted would only get worse.

It wouldn't be until the creation of the Municipality of Metropolitan Toronto in 1953, an organization that was created by the province and was given wider powers and more sources to fund such expensive projects, that a serious attempt was made to restart the project. Interestingly, even as new ideas started to evolve Toronto Mayor Allan Lamport made the following prophetic statement after warning that his city's taxpayers could not afford to pay the now more than $30 million needed to build the new waterfront highway. He suggested that it would be best to ensure that the new superhighway be made a toll road and perhaps even turn its ownership and maintenance over to private interests.

As Toronto wrestles with what it should do with the Gardiner, some old-timers can be heard to say that had we listened to good old Lampy, we wouldn't be in this pickle.

# OFFICIAL OPENING CEREMONY

## THE FREDERICK G. GARDINER EXPRESSWAY

BY

THE HONOURABLE LESLIE M. FROST, Q.C., LL.D., D.C.L.
PRIME MINISTER OF THE PROVINCE OF ONTARIO

FRIDAY, AUGUST 8TH, 1958

The first section of Toronto's new Frederick G. Gardiner Expressway, from the Humber River to Jameson Avenue, was officially opened on August 8, 1958, by Ontario Prime Minister Leslie Frost. The fourth and last section of the expressway, from York Street east connecting with the new Don Valley Parkway, opened five years and three months later. The sketch that appears on this Official Opening invitation shows the new bridges over the Humber River. The construction of these structures was the main obstacle in getting the highway project underway. Since the Humber was regarded as a navigable river it was subject to lengthy discussions and special regulations.

In early 1958 Metropolitan Toronto Chairman Fred Gardiner (gesturing), after whom the expressway was officially named on July 29, 1957, and other local and provincial politicians gathered at Fort York to discuss what impact the proposed route of the elevated expressway might have on the city's pre-eminent historic site. Some suggested the fort be moved back down to the water's edge "where it was originally located," obviously unaware that when the fort was built in the late 1700s the water lapped at its south ramparts. That delusional plan was thankfully rejected, and a slight deviation in the highway's route was made instead.

# T.O.'s Evolving Skyline

## December 30, 2012

As we enter a new year, I thought it might be both fun and informative to look back at Toronto's skyline and see how it's changed over the years. Many call it progress. Incidentally, the last photo in the trio was taken earlier this year by Jeff Clarke, an avid photographer, amateur historian, and all-round nice guy.

(Above) In this postcard view the first two towers of the Toronto-Dominion Centre in the financial heart of the city dominate the Toronto skyline. The first (fifty-six storeys) was completed in 1967, the second (forty-six storeys) three years later. The complex now consists of six towers. Still visible are the Royal York Hotel and the Bank of Commerce. In the foreground is the rather drab Terminal Warehouse (completed in 1926) that was converted into a mall/shopping/condominium complex in 1983 and renamed Queen's Quay Terminal.

(Left) This photo was taken in the early 1930s with the Royal York Hotel (which opened in 1929) and the Bank of Commerce (now Commerce Court North) at 25 King Street West dominating the skyline. The bank was built between 1929 and 1931 and when completed towered 34 floors (145 metres) over the city. Visible to the right of the same view is the spire of St. James Cathedral (93 metres), which upon its completion in 1874 was the tallest point in the city (and in fact the tallest church spire in the entire country). Thanks to a lantern placed in the spire it was often used by ships' captains sailing across Lake Ontario to determine the location of the Port of Toronto. On the subject of ships, the vessel heading for the East Gap is the popular SS *Chippewa*. For nearly half a century the vessel's distinctive "walking beam" engine made the craft easily identifiable as she sailed from Toronto to and from the Niagara River ports of Niagara-on-the-Lake and Queenston. *Chippewa* was ignominiously scrapped in 1939.

What can I say? Those landmark hotel and bank buildings are still there, although looking at this photo you'll just have to take my word for it. The dome stadium (it'll always be SkyDome to me) arrived on the skyline in 1989, joining the CN Tower that had opened to the public in mid-1976 after being under construction for forty months. (Jeff Clarke photo.)

# T.O.'s Little Piece of Venice

## January 6, 2013

The other day, Derek Boles, a founding member of the Toronto Railway Historical Association (www.trha.ca), reminded me that it was exactly 196 years ago last Friday that what would eventually become our city's first union station opened with the arrival of the Kingston to York (renamed Toronto in 1834) stagecoach.

This April 1917 photo shows Toronto's new Union Station under construction. It was officially opened by Edward, the Prince of Wales, during his August 1927 visit to our city. Later that same month, Edward and his brother Prince George dedicated the new Princes' Gates (thus the plural possessive of the word "Prince") at the east end of the CNE grounds.

While all levels of government and the nation's railways argued constantly during the construction of the city's new Union Station, the CPR threw in the towel and went ahead with building its own station on the east side of Yonge Street at the base of the escarpment south of St. Clair Avenue. It opened in June 1916. Once the new Union Station was ready, the CPR abandoned its Yonge Street building for the new station. After several years of painstaking restoration, the former CPR North Toronto station has new life as the LCBO's pre-eminent outlet. Its clock tower was based on St. Mark's Campanile in Venice.

Although the term "union station" refers to a structure where passenger trains operated by at least two different railway companies arrive and depart (for example, Toronto's Union Station with VIA and GO Transit as tenants), Derek suggests "union station" could also have referred to the arrival and departure of the transportation marvel of the early 1800s: the horse-drawn stagecoach.

This pioneer union station was located at the Church, Wellington, and Front intersection and was known by some as the Coffin Block because of its wooden construction and coffin-like shape. Over time it became the terminal for other stagecoach companies that provided service to towns and villages in the Niagara area as well as to and from the small communities scattered along Yonge Street north of York. In this role the building could truly be defined as our city's first union station. This historic structure was demolished in the early 1890s and replaced shortly thereafter by another structure that has become one of the city's true landmarks, the Flatiron, or, more correctly, Gooderham Building.

Today, the term "union station" almost always refers to a railway terminal, although the "union" designation still requires at least two railway companies to operate out of it. Here in Toronto we have had two such stations: the first opened in 1858 and was located on the old waterfront southwest of the present York and Front streets corner, while the second, a much larger facility, was erected on the site of the first in 1873. To accommodate ever increasing rail travel, the building was expanded on several occasions and served the public until the present Union Station finally went into full operation (after lengthy war-related delays, government incompetence, and the completion of the cross-waterfront railway viaduct) in 1930.

# Identified Flying Object

## January 20, 2013

When my copy of the February 2013 edition of *Popular Mechanics* arrived in the mail the other day I nearly fell off my chair when I saw the magazine's cover. I knew there was something familiar about the image that appeared under the headline "DECLASSIFIED: FLYING SAUCER REVEALED: SECRET U.S. PROGRAM".

Taking a closer look at the photo it became obvious to me that the flying saucer the magazine was trumpeting was in fact *Canada's* flying saucer. The very one that John "Jack" Frost and a few others at the Avro Canada factory adjacent to Malton Airport (now Toronto Pearson) were working on at about the same time the company's legendary Avro Arrow was still enjoying its short-lived successes.

While the Arrow was exciting much of the aviation world's experts, Frost and his colleagues were pursuing the "circular wing" concept using a discovery made by Romanian researcher Henri Coanda back in the early 1900s. Coanda had confirmed that jets of air can be bent down towards the ground using by flaps and blowing over the curved surface of the top of a wing, thereby providing vertical lift. Frost was convinced that his flying saucer, officially known as Avro Canada's Project Y2, would revolutionize transportation by air. Some aviation experts even predicted that Frost's concept would make the recently perfected helicopter type of aircraft obsolete.

A rare photo of the highly secret Avrocar undergoing one of its several less-than-successful "flights" at the Avro Canada factory adjacent to Malton Airport (now Toronto Pearson). At least the pilot appears to be pleased with what was going on.

Experimental testing of a prototype craft (weighing almost three tons) began in November 1959. Unfortunately, after months of trial flights the craft never got more than a metre off the tarmac outside one of Avro Canada's giant (and now demolished) hangars, nor did it exceed fifty-five kilometres per hour in flight. And when it got up to speed the craft would wobble, often violently.

Word about Frost's supposedly top secret project eventually got out, and when the Canadian government and Avro officials refused to continue funding and the British Ministry of Defence showed no interest, the American government and the United States Air Force stepped in, still believing that Frost was on to something. More testing was undertaken, although now at facilities south of the border. But once again it became apparent that Frost's concept wasn't going to work. The project was cancelled in 1961.

The two prototype craft were retained, with one now stored in packing cases at the U.S. Army Transportation Museum in Virginia. The other is on display at the USAF Museum at the Wright-Patterson airbase near Dayton, Ohio. All plans, photos, and reports were put into cardboard boxes and into storage. This material was eventually forwarded to the National Declassification Center in Maryland where in September of last year it was made available to researchers and historians. Thanks to *Popular Mechanics* its readers know about Avro Canada, Jack Frost, and his belief in flying saucers.

(Above) A more successful Avro Canada creation, and one that Jack Frost also worked on, was the CF-100 jet fighter. The prototype aircraft first flew sixty-three years ago yesterday. A total of 692 CF-100s were built.

(Left) The cover of the latest edition of *Popular Mechanics* features the curious Canadian-designed and -built "flying saucer" dubbed the Avrocar.

# Toronto's Master Sleuth

## January 27, 2013

One of the fun things about writing this column comes from the fact that every once in a while a letter arrives in which the sender asks me to identify an old photo that accompanies the letter. This is exactly what happened several months ago. The photograph about which the reader was asking was quite small and had been found in an old family scrapbook. With no writing anywhere on the front or back of the photo that would help identify the location, the answer to the reader's question at first appeared to be an impossible task. Particularly since the streets didn't look like any place familiar to me, even though I have wandered the city streets on foot or by car for many years. And the sign for that other city newspaper was absolutely no help.

Then, a week or so ago my wife and I paid a visit to my doctor's office for one of those annual thirty-point inspections. Richard Choi's office is in the medical building on the south side of Bloor Street just east of the Jane intersection. Parking the car in the city lot on a side street east of Jane Street, we made our way to the traffic light where we would cross Bloor and make our way to Dr. Choi's building. As I stood at the corner waiting for the light to change I suddenly had a flashback to that old photo. Could the sweeping curve followed by today's modern Bloor Street west of Jane be the same curve followed by the narrow road depicted in the old photo?

At first glance there's not much in this view to help identify it. But, after some serious sleuthing, it turns out to be a view taken looking west on Bloor Street past the Jane Street intersection. The year is still in question.

When I got home I arranged to meet with a friend who has an extremely powerful magnifying device, and upon closer examination of the photo I was able decipher the word "Jane" on the globe covering the street light at the extreme right of the view. And in the distance I was able to see a large sign that read "HUMBER VALLEY SURVEYS", a reference to Robert Home Smith's land development projects in the vicinity of today's Old Mill Inn and Spa. In front of that big sign is a much smaller one that reads, I'm pretty sure, "SWANSEA". So there's the proof. The view looks west from the Bloor and Jane corner. Now, as to the year, I can't make out that car's license plate, but my guess is sometime in the 1920s.

On closer inspection of the modern-day view we can see the familiar shape of the old Odeon Humber Theatre. That building, a favourite with residents of the Bloor West Village and nearby Swansea communities, has occupied the north side of Bloor Street since its official opening in 1949. In fact, and here's a real history twist, that opening took place exactly sixty-four years ago today (see the ad). It was the fifth of five Odeon theatres (Fairlawn, Danforth, Hyland, Toronto — later renamed Carlton — and Humber) that were scattered around our city. All but the Humber have vanished, and while it nearly suffered the same fate it was rescued and now operates as a multiplex theatre known as the Humber Cinemas.

(Above) A similar view taken early in January 2013. Note the theatre in the centre background. For more than a half-century it was the popular Odeon Humber. Thankfully, it continues to live on as the Humber Cinemas.

(Left) This newspaper ad appeared on this very day in 1949. It announced the official opening of Toronto's fifth Odeon theatre, the Odeon Humber.

# The Best-Laid Plans ...

## February 3, 2013

There's no subject that appears with more consistency on Toronto City Council's agenda than the question of what can be done to improve the GTA's worsening traffic situation. For almost as long as Torontonians have been heading to work each morning and returning home each evening, people have been faced with what is the best way to improve what is fast approaching commuter bedlam.

One of the first proposals put forward to help ease Toronto's early traffic problems was suggested in the early 1900s by a British concern that tried to convince Toronto city fathers that a monorail line shuttling back and forth high above Yonge Street was an obvious answer. What is obvious is that nothing happened with that idea.

A few years later local city politicians, having seen the success that "tube lines" (underground subways) were having in several large European and American cities, tried to convince the voters that it was time Toronto joined their ranks. While many voters agreed, the money just wasn't there (sound familiar, Mr. Mayor?). Again, nothing happened to improve the traffic situation.

More years passed, and the city streets and streetcars continued to become more and more crowded. Finally the TTC, which had been legislated into being by the province in 1920 and began operations the following year, began flexing its muscles. On January 22, 1942, TTC

The TTC's predecessor, the Toronto Railway Company, offered this solution to just what to do with its passengers' baby strollers: hang them on a hook at the back of the street-car. The TTC's decision as to how to handle today's stroller problem is expected later this month or in early March.

officials announced that while the successful outcome of the war was still very much in doubt, there was absolutely no doubt that when hostilities finally did come to an end traffic would be worse than ever. So to be sure that the city would have a plan ready for implementation as soon as the time was right, the TTC put forward a comprehensive transit improvement plan valued at $42 million.

This plan included two rapid transit lines, with the first and most important being a north-south subway under Yonge and Bay streets with terminals at Front Street and St. Clair Avenue. The second would be a dedicated streetcar right-of-way located north of and parallel to Queen Street (open-cut in places) that would connect Strachan Avenue on the west and Logan Avenue on the east. This line would use the Commission's existing PCC streetcars that had only recently been introduced on the Queen Street surface route.

What made this proposal even more interesting was the idea of adding feeder streetcar lines at the extremities of the two rapid transit lines. They would serve commuters living in the outlying communities near Eglinton and Dufferin and St. Clair and Bathurst as well as those in the west central part of town. Another streetcar feeder line would connect with the Queen route at the Don River and run north up the valley to the corner of

Broadview and Danforth. It would act as a relief line (where have I heard that term before?), taking some of the pressure off the Yonge-Bay subway.

Getting through the war successfully obviously took precedence, and while some rapid transit planning continued no actual work was undertaken until September 8, 1949, when work finally began on Toronto's (and Canada's) first subway.

Had the 1942 TTC plan been approved this is what an artist suggested that the downtown stretch of the subway along Queen Street would look like. That's the Canada Life Building on University Avenue in the centre background flanked on the south by the Old City Hall clock tower. The tallest building in the country at the time, the towering Bank of Commerce building on King Street, is to the extreme right. In the foreground, Simcoe and St. Patrick streets intersect with Queen Street. Also, note that instead of subway trains plans called for modified city streetcars.

# T.O. Tried Its Luck Before

## February 10, 2013

So what's all this chatter about a casino for Toronto? Many long-time residents of our fair city will recall a time when there were at least two such attractions by that name. The first was located on the south side of Queen Street opposite Toronto's present City Hall. It opened in 1936 as a popular burlesque and vaudeville house. Under the direction of Murray Little, the theatre's format was drastically changed in the late 1940s when he began presenting well-known Hollywood personalities as well as popular singing stars. Torontonians were entertained by such screen stars as Van Johnson, Chico Marx (one of the Marx Brothers), Gordon MacRae, Mickey Rooney, Dorothy Lamour, Bob Alda (Alan Alda's father), Basil Rathbone (Sherlock Holmes), and Huntz Hall ("Satch" of Bowery Boys' fame). Popular songsters included the Andrew Sisters, Toronto's Crew Cuts and Four Lads, Patti Page, Vaughn Monroe, Ella Fitzgerald, Eddie Fisher, Ink Spots, Rudy Vallée, Dick Todd (the "Canadian Bing Crosby"), Tex Ritter, Tony Bennett, The Platters, Johnny Rae, Winnipeg's Gisele MacKenzie, and Arthur Godfrey's Julius La Rosa. The big bands of Pee Wee Hunt, Jimmy and Tommy Dorsey, Louis Armstrong, and Count Basie also stopped by. Victor Borge's first Canadian performance was at Toronto's casino, while Bill Haley and His Comets introduced local teenagers to live rock and roll. Olsen and Johnson,

The Casino was a popular attraction visited by thousands attending the annual CNE. In this undated photo, "Bill Beasley's CASINO" was located in the Grandstand that burned down in 1946. It was replaced in time for the 1948 edition of the Ex by a fourth structure that was demolished in 1999.

the Three Stooges (including Curly), and Henny Youngman ("Take my wife, please") had Torontonians rollin' in the Casino's aisles.

With the advent of television and inexpensive trips to Las Vegas, Murray Little's Casino lost its local appeal. After a less-than-successful stint as a foreign film/fine arts cinema known as the Civic Square Theatre, this Toronto entertainment landmark was demolished in the late 1950s and the site eventually occupied by a portion of the sprawling Sheraton Centre.

With one casino up on Queen Street, Torontonians had a second place called the Casino they could visit down in the CNE grounds. However, this one was only open during the annual fairs held in the late 1930s until 1941 when the CNE was cancelled and the grounds and buildings, including the Grandstand that was built in 1907 and in which the Casino was located, were taken over by the military.

The CNE Casino featured pin games, mechanical crane machines, and other coin-operated devices and was run by Toronto-born William Beasley. Bill got his start at the 1932 CNE when he ran a dance hall in the former Transportation Building Exhibition (which, as the Spanish Pavilion, burned to the ground in 1974), bringing in such big band icons as Rudy Vallée, Duke Ellington, and Canada's Guy Lombardo. He also introduced CNE visitors to the game of Bingo and opened Toronto's first nightclub,

The popular Casino Theatre was located on Queen Street West opposite New City Hall. Today's sprawling Sheraton Centre hotel now occupies the site.

the Club Esquire on Lake Shore Boulevard at Parkside adjacent to the popular Sunnyside Amusement Park. Beasley was also one of Canada's best-known racing stable owners with his Canadian Champ winning the 1956 Queen's Plate, the first Plate event held at the new Woodbine track in Etobicoke. William Beasley died in 1968, and his grandson Bill now operates Centreville and Far Enough Farm on Toronto Islands.

# Starter Motors

## February 17, 2013

While the present Canadian International Auto Show dates from 1974, it certainly wasn't the first event to offer citizens a look at the latest in "horseless carriages." After scanning a number of old Toronto newspapers I'm pretty sure that the very first version of what we now know as an automobile show was presented April 23–30, 1904 (!!) in the brand new showroom of the Canadian Cycle & Motor Company. This building was located at what CCM described in its ads as "Automobile Corner," specifically the northeast corner of Bay and Temperance streets (just north of the ruins of the great fire that destroyed much of lower Bay Street just a couple of weeks before).

This show was certainly a modest event with something called a Peerless promoted as the main feature. Interestingly, the advertisement was aimed at visitors to the city who had come to town to attend that year's Toronto Horse Show. "They should enliven their interest in Automobiles by taking in this horseless show" the ad suggested. While this event was described as "Toronto's first Automobile Show," in reality it was a promotional event put on by just one manufacturer, the Canada Cycle & Motor Company. It wasn't until two years later that a group of automobile distributors got together and presented, for the public's enjoyment, a special week-long (March 31 to April 7, 1906) show in the two large curling rinks located behind the Granite Club on the east side

The Russell automobile was a big hit with visitors dropping by the car show in the new Transportation Building at the 1912 edition of the Canadian National Exhibition.

of Church Street north of Wellesley (the club moved to St. Clair Avenue West in the mid-1920s and to Bayview Avenue in 1972). For this show, one of the buildings featured thirty different makes of cars — Canadian, American, and foreign — while the other rink had a large display of automobile accessories and even a few motorboats.

There was enough public interest in this event that a second show was presented the following week (April 9–14) at the Mutual Street rink, with "the greatest collection of English and French automobiles ever seen together outside of the London and Paris shows."

As the years went by, the public took a greater and greater interest in the automobile and additional shows were presented, with the most popular taking place during the annual CNE. The first was in 1909 in the Transportation Building (which, as the Spanish Pavilion, burned to the ground in 1974). From 1929 on the show took over the newly

## FORD

**6-CYLINDER TOURING CAR, $3,200.**

The six cylinders of Model " K " give three impulses to every revolution of the shaft and transmit a more steady flow of power to the wheels than any Touring Car ever built.

The great surplus of energy makes possible the operation of the car at all speeds without transmitting power through several changes of gear.

See this Car, the Ford Family Touring Car at $1,100 and the Ford 4-cylinder Runabout at $650 at the Toronto Automobile Show,

## GRANITE RINK,

*.. Toronto Salesroom for the Ford Cars.*

## Dominion Automobile Co.

—— CORNER BAY AND TEMPERANCE STREETS. ——

The curling rink adjacent to the Granite Club at 519 Church Street was the site of Toronto's 1906 automobile show.

built Automotive Building (now the Allstream Centre). This extremely popular show lasted until 1967, when CNE officials decided that because the newest models didn't appear in the car showrooms around town until well after the CNE was over, the display of last year's models had become redundant. It would be another seven years before another major new car show would be presented to the public, the one that has evolved into today's Canadian International Car Show.

# T.O.'s Second Subway

## February 24, 2013

With all the talk these days about whether Toronto wants or should get subways or light rail lines (forget where the money's coming from for a moment), it's interesting to look back one half-century this very week when on February 28, 1963, citizens got the chance to ride the city's second subway line. The decision to extend the city's (and country's) pioneer subway from Union Station west to University Avenue then north and west again to a terminus at Bloor and St. George streets wasn't without its detractors. Many thought an east-west line under Bloor and the Danforth should take precedence.

It was successfully argued, however, that such a decision would put unbearable pressures on the Yonge Street line, which, while in service for a mere seven years, was already approaching full capacity at rush hour. A second north-south relief line that could help transfer passengers crowding the packed streetcars travelling along Bloor and the Danforth to and from the heart of the city was a much better choice.

While the University line operated at a loss for several years after its opening on February 28, 1963, it did prompt the city and provincial governments to expedite the construction of the first phase of the city's third subway (Keele to Woodbine), resulting in its opening almost exactly three years later, on February 26, 1966. This line crossed the Don Valley using the lower deck incorporated in the 1914 design

University Avenue looking north to Queen Street in 1956. Note the presence of the South African War Memorial in the centre boulevard. To the left of the view is the digni-fied Canada Life Building topped by its weather beacon, which was added to the original building in 1951.

of the bridge. This innovative feature was initially proposed not by Works Commissioner R.C. Harris nor by his American consultants (one of those historic fallacies), but by members of the Riverdale Businessmen's Association in 1909!

One of the factors that had to be taken into consideration prior to starting construction of the new subway was the presence of several major obstacles along the route. The most obvious was the 1,000-ton, 42-metre-high South African War Memorial located in the centre boulevard just north of the University Avenue and Queen Street intersection. Created by Toronto sculptor Walter Allward (who is also responsible for the Canadian National Vimy Memorial in France) the work recognized those Canadians who had lost their lives in what was known far and wide as simply the Boer War, 1899–1902. It was erected at a cost of $40,000 in 1910, with the bronze figure representing both Peace and Mother Canada at the apex added in 1911.

The original location of the monument was on the east side of a narrower University Avenue. When the city decided to widen the street in the late 1940s, and in so doing to separate the existing

A similar view, circa 1961. Note that in this photo the South African War Memorial that had stood in the boulevard just north of Queen Street is missing. It would be replaced upon completion of the new subway under University Avenue.

In this 1917 picture, workers building the Bloor Street Viaduct across the Don Valley (renamed the Prince Edward Viaduct two years later following the prince's visit in 1919) pose for the photographer. In the same view we can see the outline of a lower deck designed and incorporated in the structure to accommodate a future subway that opened nearly a half-century later.

north-south traffic lanes by a centre boulevard, it became necessary to move Allward's work. With the sculptor supervising, the monument was moved in one piece to a new location and then onto a concrete base in the new centre boulevard.

A decade passed, and when it was decided to build the new University subway using the cut-and-cover method south of "hospital row" (quieter tunnelling would be used in the vicinity of the hospitals and northward under the Parliament Buildings) it was obvious that once again Allward's monument would have to be moved. However, Allward had passed away, and rather than taking a chance on another stressful (and now unsupervised) move, engineers began looking for the original plans used to assemble the monument from individual pieces of stone. Once the plans were found the structure was literally taken apart and the individual pieces removed to an off-site location and stored. Once work was complete the monument was reassembled, apparently no worse for wear.

# A Real Swinger on Bathurst

## March 3, 2013

We usually reserve anniversaries as an occasion to celebrate important people (February 25, 1752, the birthday of our community's founder, John Graves Simcoe), important events (May 2, 1967, the last time the Maple Leafs hockey team won the Stanley Cup), or the opening of a city landmark (September 18, 1899, the opening of Toronto's Old City Hall).

Interestingly, March 3 marks the anniversary of one of the more unusual of our many city landmarks: the massive bridge that carries traffic over the railway tracks near the south end of Bathurst Street. However, let me be clear, the anniversary I've selected is not the date that this particular bridge was first opened over that busy rail corridor, but rather the date of a minor (at least from our modern-day perspective) engineering accomplishment that would change the bridge's point of view for all time. Here's the rest of the story.

In the city's earliest days the waters of Toronto Bay lapped at the southernmost ramparts of what we know today as Fort York. Bathurst Street, so named for the 3rd Earl Bathurst, Secretary for War and the Colonies (1812–1837), was a simple dirt pathway that ran from the westernmost end of Front Street (so named as it delineated the front of the Town of York) north to Lot (now Queen) Street. Here it changed names, becoming Cruikshank's Lane, a term that recognized the nearby estate of the Honourable George Cruikshank.

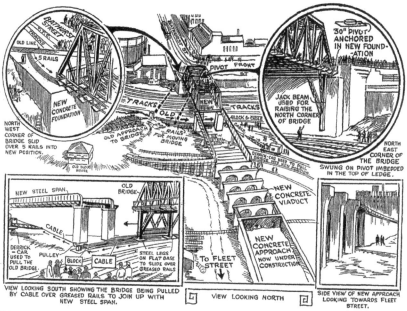

This newspaper sketch shows the realignment of the Bathurst Street bridge, an engineering triumph that took place in just fifteen minutes.

When the land south and east of the old fort was eventually reclaimed from the old bay the railways quickly put down their tracks, thereby obstructing pedestrians from an easy and safe access to their waterfront. This action would haunt the city for decades to come. When the city fathers decided to extend Bathurst Street south of Front Street it was necessary to erect a new bridge to allow horse-drawn carts and pedestrians to cross the railway corridor safely. However, preventing the construction of this bridge in a north-south direction was the fact that several factories had been erected south of the Bathurst and Front intersection. This forced the Grand Trunk Railway (GTR) to build its new Bathurst Street bridge, a relatively simple steel structure with wood decking, in a slightly skewed southwest-northeast direction, forcing traffic to proceed along the southernmost edge of the old fort.

When city officials decided that a more direct route to and from the annual CNE was needed, they selected Bathurst Street as that route. However, the streetcars were far too heavy for the old bridge. There was no question that it had to be replaced with a more robust structure. In an effort to save the taxpayers some money, an anonymous GTR railway

The present Bathurst Street bridge over the railway tracks south of Front Street didn't start its long "career" in that location. It was built in 1903 as a railway bridge over the Humber River just north of the old Lakeshore Road. This is a photograph of the original builder's plaque on that bridge. Thirteen years later the 1903 structure was disassembled and the sections removed to the foot of Bathurst Street where they were reassembled. This "new" bridge replaced an old bridge that crossed the railway tracks at an angle and had been deemed unsafe. Some years later a plan was devised to straighten Bathurst Street and extended it south to connect with Fleet Street (now Lake Shore Boulevard West). As part of this interesting engineering project the former Humber River bridge was realigned in a new north-south direction as it is today.

official suggested that the company's soon-to-be-demolished railway bridge that had been erected in 1903 over the Humber River just north of the Lakeshore Road would be a perfect replacement. With all in agreement, that bridge was disassembled and shipped in pieces to the foot of Bathurst Street, where it was quickly reassembled and available for streetcar traffic in time for the 1916 edition of the CNE.

But the Bathurst Street bridge continued to impede the ever increasing number of cars and pedestrians making their way to and from the CNE's recently developed East Entrance or to and from the Maple Leaf Stadium on Fleet Street (now Lake Shore Boulevard). What to do? The GTR engineers had an idea. Rather than take the bridge apart once again and rebuild it so that it faced north-south, they would simply build a pivot point under the bridge's northeast corner, hook a huge steam engine to the south end of the 750-ton bridge, and pull it through an arc of twenty-six degrees. The move took a mere fifteen minutes. A steel span was then built south of the repositioned bridge, and soon traffic flowed smoothly between Lake Shore Boulevard and Front Street, just as it does (well, sort of) today.

# Gargoyles Get a Second Life

## March 10, 2013

There was a time when our city had a substantial collection of fine old buildings: the University Avenue Armouries, the Registry Building across from today's Old City Hall, the Temple Building at Bay and Richmond, and the Bank of Toronto's head office at Bay and King, to name just a few. All of these, plus many more, vanished in copious clouds of dust as the city rushed to modernize and, in the process, many hoped, create a new New York City.

While work on Toronto's second purpose-built City Hall was almost complete at the top of Bay Street construction crews anxiously awaited the delivery of the tower clock mechanism and trio of bells that were still in transit from the Gillett and Johnston foundry in England. The reason for the late delivery was the delayed arrival at the company office of the city's purchase order. When the components did arrive they were hoisted up the outside of the tower and into their final resting positions, through the south-facing clock face opening. Note the original gargoyles that were removed in the early 1930s and replaced with "replicas" during a major restoration of the building in 2003.

Thankfully, one structure that survived the onslaught of the 1960s and 70s was Toronto's former municipal building at Queen and Bay streets. Initially promoted as a combined courthouse and city hall complex, the $2.5-million structure designed by Toronto's prolific and talented architect Edward James Lennox opened in the fall of 1899. The building was dominated by a massive ninety-metre-high tower, which would eventually feature a massive clock that would peel with Westminster chimes.

Another rather unusual feature of the tower was the presence of four massive gargoyles carved out of New Brunswick sandstone and affixed in place just below the clock face. There they remained until city officials ordered the quartet removed for safety reasons. Time, weather, and the soft and porous nature of the sandstone had all contributed to the deterioration of the figures. In fact, on two separate occasions large pieces had crashed to the ground. The gargoyles had to go.

# The Fileys Head South

## March 24, 2013

A little over a week before writing this column I asked my wife of almost forty-five years if she'd like to take a trip south. "Of course," she answered. "When?"

The newest in public transportation vehicles undergoes testing at the 1885 edition of the Toronto Industrial Exhibition, an event officially known since 1912 as the Canadian National Exhibition. A special feature of this experiment was the trolley pole, a new device that was used to collect electricity from an overhead wire. Previous experiments worldwide had used a third rail system, an expensive (and more importantly dangerous) method.

It was 2:15 in the morning on March 15 when my wife Yarmila got this photo of 4400 as it headed out the Hillcrest gate at the start of its trip to the CNE loop.

"Be ready to leave early Friday morning," was my reply. So at precisely 1:01 a.m. we headed out, and by 1:30 we had arrived opposite the TTC's Hillcrest shops between Dupont and Davenport on the west side of Bathurst Street.

So why did I say we were going south? We live in Willowdale, and that's south for us.

To my wife's credit, I'm pretty sure she knew exactly what I had in mind for that morning. A week or so earlier I had mentioned to Yarmila that word had gotten out that the TTC's new streetcar, 4400, would make its inaugural run from the Hillcrest complex to the streetcar loop at the CNE, where a number of tests would be conducted. I thought it would be neat from a historical perspective to follow 4400 along the route just as an earlier collection of Toronto streetcar buffs must have done when the then state-of-the-art Peter Witt and PCC models hit the streets, the former back in the early 1920s and the latter in the late 1930s. Oh, and the fact we didn't pack any luggage was another good hint.

While we sat in the car awaiting the start of the historic trip, a police car pulled up beside us. The young officer asked if we were lost. "No, we aren't," I replied.

"What are you doing sitting in the car this time of the morning?" (He obviously didn't realize we have been married for almost half a century.)

The first of the TTC's 204 new streetcars "poses" in the Hillcrest shop alongside the TTC's venerable 1923 Peter Witt. It's anticipated that Witt 2766 (the last of more than 350 Witt motors that were once part of the TTC fleet) were featured in the Beaches Easter Parade along Queen Street East the year this photo was taken. Joining it was one of the two remaining PCC Streamliners, 4500 and 4549, which were built in 1951. Introduced in 1938 were a grand total of 745 PCCs (new and used), the last one being retired from revenue service in 1995. (Photo courtesy John Smatlak.)

Not missing a beat I replied, "Would you believe we're waiting for a streetcar?" We quickly went on to explain what was happening, and with that the officers took off, entering the TTC yard to get a look for themselves. Yarmila and I sat back to continue the wait.

# Historic and Truly Moving

## March 31, 2013

During its 150 years of existence on the north side of Duke (renamed Adelaide Street East when Adelaide and Duke were joined at the Jarvis Street intersection) at the top of Frederick, the old house at number 64 had a wide variety of occupants. They included elevator manufacturers, electricians, glass companies, printers, horseshoe nail makers, and, in its earliest

The move of the old house from the corner of Adelaide and Frederick streets in the old Town of York began early Good Friday morning exactly forty-one years ago today. The two-hundred-ton structure arrived (with all its bricks in place) just north of the Queen and University intersection (as seen in this photo) later that same day. It was here the house rested until moved onto the south lawn of the Canada Life Building the following day.

Erected in 1822 as William Campbell's new residence in the Town of York, the house at the northwest corner of Queen Street East and University Avenue is now a museum and home of the Advocates' Society.

Sir William Campbell served as Chief Justice of the Supreme Court of the Province of Upper Canada from 1825 until he retired in 1829, the same year he was knighted. Interestingly, the seventy-six-year-old judge passed away in 1834, the same year the Town of York became the City of Toronto.

days, Toronto families. The earliest family was that of William Campbell, a Scot who came to York (renamed Toronto in 1834). He eventually attained the distinguished position of the Chief Justice of the Supreme Court.

The last occupant of the old house was Coutts-Hallmark, a greeting card manufacturer who, when room was needed to expand, offered the now 140-year-old structure to any organization on the condition that the house be moved off the property. It was then that some six hundred lawyers, members of the Advocates' Society, stepped forward and raised $500,000 to save the oldest house still standing in the original Town of York from certain demolition. That story is recorded in the photos that accompany this column.

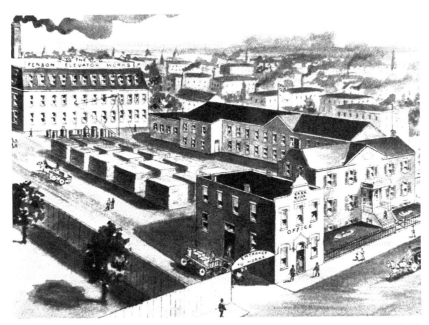

This sketch of the Fensom Elevator Works on Duke Street (now Adelaide Street East), at the top of Frederick Street, is from a circa 1904 promotional booklet. The company's main office occupied the old Campbell House visible at the extreme right. In the following year Fensom joined with Elisha Graves Otis to create the Otis-Fensom Elevator Company (in 1949 renamed the Otis Elevator Company), which today is the world's largest manufacturer of vertical transportation systems.

# Jets Back on Island Radar

## April 14, 2013

As many readers will attest, I frequently select a subject for these columns based on some special anniversary. Such is the case for today's feature, the eighty-sixth anniversary, to the day, of when what was known as the Toronto Transportation Commission (since 1954 the Toronto Transit Commission) took over full operation of the city's ferryboats that plied the waters of Toronto Bay to and from a trio of Toronto Islands destinations: Ward's Island, Centre Island, and Hanlan's Point.

Prior to April 14, 1927, that important public service had been handled by the Toronto Ferry Co., a private enterprise that over the years had brought together a small collection of individual companies in an attempt to improve the service that, because of the ever increasing number of visitors to Toronto's island oasis, had gotten out of control. Frequently, the company that transported people to the Islands on a prepaid return trip basis would vanish, leaving the visitor to pay extra for a return fare. The Toronto Ferry Co. solved this problem but was reluctant to spend the thousands of dollars necessary to upgrade a fleet of vessels that were well past their prime. That fact, combined with the transfer of the popular pro baseball team from the Hanlan's Point stadium to a modern stadium on the mainland and the resulting loss of huge numbers of fans using the private operator's ferryboats, led to the city having to accept the responsibility for all Islands passenger service.

This undated photo features a rare aerial view of Hanlan's Point and the adjacent sand-bar. Toronto's new airport would be built on this site and was initially given the title Port George VI Airport, a name that vanished very soon after the king's visit in the spring of 1939. The second airport built at the same time, miles out of town near the farming community of Malton (eventually renamed Toronto Pearson), was a secondary facility to be used in case fog shut down the main island facility.

One of the TTC's new Peter Witt streetcars pauses at the old Toronto Ferry Docks (then between Bay and York streets) just days after April 14, 1927, the date that the TTC officially took over all ferryboat operations from the privately operated Toronto Ferry Co. Note the daily parking rate was 25¢. The adult fare to the Islands was two streetcar tickets at 7¢ each, both deposited when boarding at the mainland. One ticket was for crossing the bay and the other for the return voyage.

On April 14, 1927, that job was officially turned over to the six-year-old TTC, which added a number of vessels (including the 1890 *Mayflower* and *Primrose*, the 1906 *Bluebell*, and the 1910 *Trillium*, the latter still in active service after a million-dollar restoration carried out nearly thirty years ago) to its existing roster of streetcars and buses.

As mentioned in this column's first paragraph, the acquisition of the Islands ferry service by the TTC (something that lasted until Metro Toronto took over ferry operations in 1962) was to be the sole subject of this week's feature. Then along came the surprise announcement that Porter Airlines had acquired a number of Bombardier's new CS100 passenger jet aircraft. This immediately prompted the question of whether jet aircraft of

## Jets seen using Island airport in '72

Toronto's Island Airport may be enlarged to handle jet airliners within five years, it was confirmed today.

Preliminary studies by the Toronto Harbor Commission, which controls the airport, envision a waterfront jetport for the proposed billion-dollar transport and business complex in the lower downtown area.

The enlarged island airport would handle only medium-range jets, leaving long-range airliners and supersonic jumbo transports to Toronto International Airport at Malton, E. B. Griffith, the Harbor Commission general manager said.

Griffith said the enlarged airport—connected by bridge or rapid transit with the mainland—would be ideal as a terminus for "airbus" transport to relatively nearby centres such as Montreal or New York.

Studies by the commission were initiated last summer and a decision on whether to seek approval for construction from the Department of Transport will likely be made by the end of the year, Griffith said.

Some government officials have already been consulted and talks have been held with major airlines, he said.

The project has been made feasible through the commission's five-year plan to route most shipping into the harbor through an enlarged eastern entrance.

Principal feature of the waterfront airport for travellers would be its proximity to Metro's business centre, Griffith said.

"Our studies show that all of this is economically feasible and it will be only 10 minutes from downtown," he said.

Present plans call for no encroachment of island parkland by the airport, Griffith said.

The existing island airport had more than 228,000 aircraft movements. Most of the present traffic involves small private, flying school or business aircraft.

The *Toronto Star* newspaper used this headline for its April 25, 1967, story. In it, officials anticipated that the Toronto Island Airport would be a Jetport within five years.

any kind (Porter's current fleet consists of turboprop Q400s) would be permitted to use the Billy Bishop Toronto City Airport facilities, which operate under the 1983 tripartite agreement that prevents the airport's use by jet aircraft.

However, in the back of my mind was something I had read that was related to an attempt to open the Island Airport for use by jet planes. After some searching I came across what had stirred my thought processes. It was a story that appeared in the city's three newspapers almost exactly forty-six years ago. The Island Airport would be a "jetport"! Obviously the suggestion put forward in this report never came to fruition. I'll bet Robert Deluce wishes it had.

# A Hot Time in the Old Town of York

### April 28, 2013

Exactly two hundred years have passed since forces arriving from south of the border invaded the little Town of York in the Province of Upper Canada (now the City of Toronto in Ontario). It was a nasty and, as history tells us, totally unnecessary affair. To honour the memory of those who helped defend our community, many with their lives, cartophile Nathan Ng has prepared a fascinating new website that features dozens of maps related to historic Fort York and its environs. Check it out at http://fortyorkmaps.blogspot.ca/.

While on the subject of the War of 1812, here are a couple of interesting particulars about that conflict that began on June 18, 1812, with the American declaration of war on Great Britain, and ended with the signing of the Treaty of Ghent on Christmas Eve, 1814. Unfortunately, the word that peace had been attained failed to arrive in time to prevent the war's final clash on January 8, 1815. That unsuccessful communication resulted in the Battle of New Orleans and the needless deaths of an additional four hundred military personnel, the vast majority of whom were British.

As part of a series of friendly "hands across the border" events during Toronto's centennial year, American president Franklin Delano Roosevelt and members of his Congress ordered that the original Mace be returned into the custody of the Province of Ontario. In this photo from the Toronto Harbour Commission Archives, the gunship USS *Wilmington* arrives in Toronto Harbour on July 5, 1934, ready to deliver the historic Mace to Lieutenant Governor Herbert Bruce at an elaborate ceremony that took place at Fort York. That event was attended by the governors of the states of New Jersey, New York, and Michigan as well as the mayors of Buffalo and Rochester (interestingly, the latter city has the same birth year as Toronto).

# Streetcar Inferno

## May 5, 2013

What follows is a story from Toronto's past that I initially wondered whether I should go ahead and include as one of my *Sunday Sun* columns. Because it concerns such a sad event, I wondered if there are any family members still around who might be upset at having the event resurrected nearly a half-century after it happened. However, I concluded that as sad as the May 3, 1946, event might have been, it still remains a part of Toronto's history. And mine as well, even though I was not quite four and half years of age when the tragedy happened. Here's the story.

It was the height of the Friday afternoon rush hour as crowds of people boarded the TTC's relatively new PCC streetcar 4076 operating on the Bloor-Danforth route at the Bathurst Street car stop. With each passenger having deposited his or her 10¢ fare (or ticket purchased three for a quarter) in the fare box or having simply handed the operator, Henry Schepers, a transfer from a Bathurst car, the doors closed and 4076 picked up speed and made its way west to the line's terminal at the Jane Street loop.

Suddenly there was a sickening crash as the front of the streetcar sliced into the cab and gas tank of a thirty-foot tractor-trailer that had suddenly appeared out of nowhere and run the north-south red light crossing in front of the streetcar. Somehow the truck had lost its brakes seconds after turning south off St. Clair Avenue and onto Bathurst

A westbound TTC streetcar on the Bloor-Danforth route sits askew in the middle of the Bathurst and Bloor intersection following a collision with a runaway tractor-trailer on May 3, 1946. Structural damage to the car was minimal; the searing gasoline-fed fire did the damage. Note the sign for one of the city's once ubiquitous Danforth Radio stores describing the various radios sold within. In the background is a portion of the marquee of the Midtown (now Bloor) Theatre. (Photo from the City of Toronto Archives.)

Street. It began picking up speed as it descended the steep hill north of Davenport Road. The driver, Murray Boyce, and his co-worker, Jack Day, realized the fifteen-ton behemoth was cascading down the street totally out of control. As the truck approached the Bathurst and Bloor intersection, having successfully traversed the Dupont Street crossing without incident, it began to slow while the driver and his helper continued to warn pedestrians and other drivers to get out of the way. Unable to get the truck stopped, the inevitable happened.

The slow-moving streetcar ripped into the truck's exposed saddle tank. Gasoline rushed out and washed through the streetcar, suddenly ignited, and within a split second flames erupted, scorching any unfortunates in their way. The hundred or so passengers screamed and raced for the rear doors, the front entrance having taken the full impact of the crash. Pedestrians alerted by the sound of the collision raced to the streetcar and began smashing windows so trapped passengers could escape the inferno taking over the interior of the car.

Within minutes the flames had burned themselves out, and while structural damage was minor because the speed of the converging vehicles was mercifully slow (in fact, only a few months passed before a refitted 4076 was returned to service) the accident and fire had claimed two lives, while dozens of others were admitted to Toronto General and Western Hospital with an assortment of burns, bruises, and cuts from the flying glass. One of the victims was a former flying instructor who had survived the war and received his official discharge from the RCAF only six months prior to the accident. The other victim had only recently learned that his son had died in an enemy prisoner-of-war camp.

While the deaths of two TTC passengers was certainly tragic, a little more than a month later the city was further saddened to learn that two more passengers had succumbed to their burns.

What makes this story more personal is the fact that I was living with my parents and younger brother, Bob, just steps away from the Bloor and Bathurst corner. While I was less than five years of age and obviously don't remember the tragedy, years later I was told that my grandmother was on the following Bloor streetcar. Would she have gotten off 4076 at Bathurst or travelled to the next stop as usual? As it turned out, the service disruption resulted in her walking the last few blocks.

# Toronto's Changing Waterfront

## May 12, 2013

As Porter Airlines works with representatives of the three jurisdictions that since 1983 have directed the uses of the Billy Bishop Toronto City Airport — the federal government, the Toronto Port Authority, and the City of Toronto — in an effort to bring jet airliner service to the airport on Toronto Islands, one of the most contentious issues affecting the negotiations is the need, for safety reasons, to extend the airport's main 1,220-metre runway east by 168 metres into Toronto Bay and by a similar length west out into Lake Ontario.

To be sure, there are other concerns about this Porter project (such as the possibility that the noise from Bombardier's new CSeries jet airliners may exceed the permitted acoustic threshold, something we won't know until one of the new planes actually takes to the air), what is interesting about the concern over lengthening the runway is that alterations to Toronto's harbour have been going on since shortly after John Graves Simcoe, the province's first lieutenant governor and the community's founder, sailed across the pristine waters of the bay to a shoreline just south of the present Front Street more than two hundred years ago!

Some of those changes were good, others not so good. But all were made in the name of business improvement and city progress. I would suggest that the jury is still out on the ultimate value of the recent influx of condominium towers across the waterfront.

The photos that accompany this column illustrate the incredible changes to the waterfront in a span of less than one hundred years. Examination of the selection of historic maps compiled by Nelson Ng (available online at oldtorontomaps.blogspot.ca/p/index-of-maps.html) further demonstrates those changes.

* After various levels of government spent years discussing the future of Captain John Letnik's floating seafood restaurant, MV *Jadran* was finally towed out of its berth in the Yonge Street slip on June 13, 2015. It was taken to a Port Colborne scrap yard where it will be cut into pieces.

The top photo shows the stretch of the city's waterfront located by the old Union Station west of the York Street bridge over the railway tracks. To the extreme right of this circa 1920 aerial view is the dangerous level crossing at Yonge Street. In the centre of the photo is Toronto's new (and present) Union Station, still not in use as it awaits the relocation of railway tracks on a new cross-waterfront viaduct. Poised on its own pier jutting out into the bay is the new Toronto Harbour Commission (THC) office building flanked by a pair of shipping company warehouses. From this vantage point THC officials were able to point out to representatives of prospective clients the advantages of opening branch manufacturing factories somewhere along the city's developing waterfront.

John McQuarrie, who took all of the contemporary photos in my book *Toronto, Then and Now*, captured this remarkable image of the central waterfront back in 2008. Queen's Quay Terminal is visible to the extreme left while to the extreme right is the Yonge Street slip, the Toronto Ferry Docks, and Captain John's seafood restaurant, the former cruise ship MV *Jadran*. As with any photo taken of the city's skyline these days, the addition of new condominium and office towers quickly dates the image.

# Floating History

## May 26, 2013

Ships of all sizes have always been important in the growth years of our nation. Many carried new Canadians west to settle the prairies, others carried recent immigrants to and from pleasure grounds for a few hours away from the stifling heat and crowded sidewalks of the nation's big cities. SS *Keewatin* is an example of the former; PS *Trillium* represents the latter.

On December 3, 1973, *Trillium* awaits the next step in a lengthy restoration process to bring the historic craft back to operating status. In the background what would soon become another city landmark takes shape.

One of oldest participants in the 2013 Doors Open celebration, an annual event that features a public look inside dozens of Toronto's most interesting buildings, isn't a building at all, but rather the Toronto Islands ferry *Trillium*. Built in 1910 at the sprawling Polson Iron Works factory at the foot of Sherbourne Street (about where the railway viaduct is located today), the $75,000 steam-powered, side-paddle vessel was the fourth of the so-called flower boats in the fleet of the privately owned Toronto Ferry Co. The others that operated between the mainland and Ward's Island, Centre Island, and Hanlan's Point were the *Mayflower*, *Primrose* (both built in 1890), and *Trillium*'s almost identical four-year-older sister, *Bluebell*. The first two vessels were scrapped by the new owner, the TTC, in the 1930s, while *Bluebell* met her end in the mid-1950s. A similar fate awaited *Trillium*, but that was not to be. She was simply abandoned in an isolated lagoon and left to rot away. In 1973, the Metro Toronto government (led by Chairman Paul Godfrey) authorized *Trillium*'s rehabilitation. After nearly three years of painstaking and loving work undertaken by a special group of craftspeople, the historic vessel with restored steam engine, rebuilt side-paddles, and, of course, updated safety systems was back on Toronto Bay. (Photo courtesy Paul Allen.)

Built by the Fairfield Shipping and Engineering Co. and launched at its Govan, Scotland, shipyard in 1907, the new Canadian Pacific passenger steamer SS *Keewatin* initially saw service between Owen Sound on Georgian Bay and Port Arthur (now part of Thunder Bay) at the head of Lake Superior. In 1912, the CPR created a new so-called super port at what is now Port McNicoll, so named to honour David McNicoll, one of CPR's vice-presidents. This was to be *Keewatin's* home port for the next fifty-five years. An interesting feature of *Keewatin's* voyage from Scotland through the Great Lakes was the fact that her 107-metre length precluded traversing the existing locks along the St. Lawrence River and the old Welland Canal, which accommodated ships that were less than 57 metres and 43 metres, respectively. As a result, *Keewatin* had to be cut in two, with each section then passing through the locks separately. The sections were reassembled at a Buffalo, New York, shipyard, then the vessel sailed on to Owen Sound. SS *Keewatin* went on to operate between first Owen Sound and later the new super port at Port McNicoll and Port Arthur at the head of Lake Superior until she was retired from service in the fall of 1966. In the spring of 2012, SS *Keewatin* was repatriated from Saugatuck, Michigan, where, saved at the last minute from eager wreckers, she had been converted to a floating museum. *Keewatin's* triumphant arrival home in Port McNicoll's harbour is captured in this remarkable photo taken by Craig White. SS *Keewatin* now welcomes visitors eager to explore the world's last Edwardian-era passenger liner. See details at www.sskeewatin.com.

# Postcard from the Wedge

## June 2, 2013

Anyone who visits the St. Lawrence Market area of our city on a regular basis will no doubt have noticed that the most photographed view of the city is the one taken from Front Street east of Church looking towards the downtown skyscrapers and past the ancient Gooderham Building. For many visitors to our city, this view, a few photographs of the CN Tower, and New City Hall are the images that they will associate with our city when they look through their scrapbooks (real or digital) in the years to come. All three of these photos were taken from approximately the same location; that is, from the south side of Front Street a few steps east of the Church Street corner.

Close inspection of the most recent of the photos that accompany this column shows the remarkable changes to the city's downtown skyline over the last 125 or so years. A few of the major buildings in the 2013 photo include the two Brookfield (formerly BCE) Place towers, the Royal Bank Plaza, one of the five TD Centre towers, Commerce Court, First Canadian Place (incidentally the tallest building in Canada), the Bay Adelaide Centre, and Scotia Plaza. And tucked in at the northwest corner of Church and Wellington streets is the former one-storey TD banking pavilion that over the last few years has served as a pizza place and still stands as a fast food eatery.

The most intriguing of the structures visible in both views is the 1892 Gooderham Building, also known, because of its distinctive shape, as the "chocolate cake" building. In fact, it's probably safe to say that it's this distinctive shape, rather than any historical or architectural reason (though they should have sufficed), that has resulted in the old building's retention. The unusual footprint of the land it stands on (described by surveyors as a "gore zone") was difficult to develop without purchasing adjacent property. After considering the building's future, developers eventually decided to simply leave it alone and look somewhere else. Today, no one would dare touch it.

This colour penny postcard features the 1892 Gooderham Building surrounded by structures that today would be considered historical keepers. Except for Gooderham's iconic office building, all of the buildings pictured have been demolished. Note the telegraph poles that carried messages from offices in Toronto to offices around the world. Telegraph service was the worldwide web of the day.

Of particular interest is this old black-and-white photo. It was taken before the construction of the Gooderham Building and shows the building that previously occupied the Church, Wellington, and Front Street site. Made of wood, this structure was known colloquially as the Coffin Block because of its distinctive casket-like shape. The old building housed one of the city's earliest telegraph offices and for a time was the western terminal of the Kingston-York (now Toronto) stagecoach service. In addition, it was from this corner that coaches bound for Hamilton and Niagara Peninsula destinations would commence their journeys. The old building was demolished when work began on the new Gooderham Building in 1891. Date unknown.

# Toronto's Early Hotels

## June 9, 2013

Visitors to the Town of York, the name of our city until it was changed to Toronto in 1834, had little to choose from when it came to selecting overnight accommodation following the establishment of the town in 1793. In fact, it's generally accepted that the community's first "hotel" was the one run by Abner Miles. Located on the north side of King Street between Ontario and Berkeley streets, the place was better known as the new town's most popular tavern, although it is recorded that provision could be made for visitors to stay the night if it was necessary.

Historically, it was Jordan's York City Hotel, which opened in 1801, that has the distinction of being the community's first real hotel. In fact, many travellers regarded it as the most fashionable place of accommodation in the entire province of Upper Canada (after 1867 known as Ontario).

As the years passed, Toronto became increasingly important as both a business centre and a tourism destination. To accommodate visitors to the city, the number of hotels and (with the advent of motor travel) motor hotels, aka motels, steadily increased. To list the names of the city's hotels, past and present, would take up most of this section of the *Sunday Sun*. However, one of them (arguably the best known) was the Queen's Hotel on the north side of Front Street between Bay and York streets. It first opened in 1862 and welcomed guests for more than six decades.

In this early 1928 photo a clutch of cars is seen angle parked facing Toronto's new, yet unopened, Union Station. On the other side of Front Street, the "ancient" Queen's Hotel has vanished and excavation proceeds on the foundation of the new $16-million Royal York Hotel. The governor general of the day, Viscount Willingdon, presided over the hotel's official opening, which took place on June 11, 1929.

In 1927 the Canadian Pacific Railway announced that the company would build the finest hotel in the country. The site that had been selected was opposite the city's massive new Union Station, then still under construction. Obviously, the Queen's would have to go, and so it was that on September 10 of that year the doors to one of the province's best known hostelries closed forever. Within a few weeks the venerable Queen's was no more.

On the last day of June 1927, just weeks before work started on excavating for the $16-million, 28-floor, 1,100-room hotel, the CPR's president, Edward W. Beatty, announced that the new structure would be known as the Royal York Hotel, a proud reference to the name the city's founder, John Graves Simcoe, gave the town in 1793 when he called it the Royal Town of York.

The new hotel was officially opened on June 11, 1929, by the governor general of the day, Viscount Willingdon.

Construction of the Royal York's 7-floor, 400-room addition began in 1957 and was ready for guests two years later.

# The Little Tug That Could

## June 23, 2013

Sharp-eyed visitors to this year's Canadian National Exhibition (August 16–September 2) will notice that another long-time attraction on the fairgrounds is missing. Constructed in 1932 by the Toronto Drydock Company in its yard on the Keating Channel (the short waterway that connects the Don River with Toronto Bay, named in honour of City Engineer Edward Keating, who served from 1892 until 1898), the company's 184-ton, 23-metre-long tug *Ned Hanlan* would go on to serve the City of Toronto Works Department, and after 1953 the Metro Toronto Works Department, in various capacities and as a passenger ferry and icebreaker whenever Toronto Bay froze over, something that would incapacitate the regular Islands ferryboats, until the busy little vessel was retired in 1967. After lengthy discussions the tug was moved to the CNE grounds in 1971 and put on display west of the former Marine Museum (the only structure remaining out of the numerous buildings that once made up the historic Stanley Barracks). There *Ned* remained, along with CN's steam locomotive 6213, for more than four decades. In 2009 the locomotive was moved to a more appropriate home at the Toronto Railway Museum near the CN Tower. Now *Ned* was alone.

Then late last year the tug was also given a new home near the ferry dock at Hanlan's Point, not far from the statue honouring Ned Hanlan, the world's champion sculler and the historic vessel's namesake. After years apart, Ned the athlete and *Ned* the busy little tug are finally together.

In addition to the usual things a working tug does, the little *Ned Hanlan* also provided Islanders with emergency ferry service when necessary. Here the tug enters the slip adjacent to the old Canada Steamship Line sheds at the foot of Yonge Street. (Photo from the Toronto Public Library collection.)

The tug *Ned Hanlan* sits proudly at its new home over at Hanlan's Point on Toronto Islands, where it was moved early in 2013.

In the summer of 1929 the small Islands ferry *John Hanlan* (named for Ned's father, who is the person for whom Hanlan's Point is named as well) was loaded with fireworks and old tires and set on fire in the lake south of Sunnyside Amusement Park as a "spectacle."

# Northern Fighters

## June 30, 2013

I t was on July 1, 1863, that the most horrendous battle of the more than a hundred that took place during the American Civil War began, turning life upside down for the 2,400 citizens living in and around the small community of Gettysburg, Pennsylvania. For three consecutive days, armies of the Union and the Confederacy tore each other to pieces. Over the three-day period casualties numbered more than 51,000.

While my columns almost always deal with items related to our city's history, I found it interesting to learn that several thousand citizens from the colonies in British North America, including the Province of Canada (later to be renamed the Provinces of Ontario and Quebec when the new Dominion of Canada was established 146 years ago tomorrow, exactly four years after the Battle of Gettysburg began), joined either the Union or Confederate armies.

The exact number that signed up has remained a mystery, since the British colonies were officially neutral and any citizen who signed up with a foreign army was just asking for trouble when, and if, they returned home. Nevertheless, most experts agree that the number joining the Union army could have been as high as fifty-five thousand, with a much smaller number siding with President of the Confederate States Jefferson Davis. Those fighting for the North were for the most part waging war against the appalling concept of human slavery. Those

The Queen's Hotel on the site of today's Royal York Hotel. This postcard depicts the hotel as it looked when the place served as "headquarters" for many visiting Confederate spies eager to get our country to go to war against the Union forces and to recruit much needed members for the dwindling Confederate army. It was also here that Jacob Thompson and others promoted the burning of hotels in New York City and Chicago in retaliation for the burning of Atlanta.

who joined with the South were more concerned that when Abraham Lincoln's mighty northern army eventually won the conflict he and his generals would seek retribution against Great Britain, which had been covertly aiding the South, and would quickly move to annex the mother country's North American colonies by force.

The four-year-long war, which finally came to an end on April 9, 1865, resulted in a total of 620,000 casualties.

Equally difficult is determining how many from north of the border participated during the three days of fighting in and around Gettysburg. Paul Culliton, a long-time friend and Civil War re-enactor, was able to give me details concerning one Torontonian who died on a Gettysburg battlefield. Lieutenant Robert Evans had joined the 108th New York Infantry Regiment, which was formed in Rochester in July 1862. He was one of 102 members of the regiment killed or wounded at Gettysburg, having been shot in the head by a sharpshooter on the second day of the battle. Is he among the 3,500 Union soldiers buried in the Gettysburg National Military Cemetery? Wish I knew.

The horrors of the American Civil War were still in the minds of many Torontonians when in November 1889 the Battle of Gettysburg was presented at the city's art gallery located on the south side of Front Street west of York. Known as the Cyclorama, this circular building featured huge, panoramic paintings of various historical events. In later years the building was repurposed as a machinery showroom, then parking garage, then demolished. The Citiplace office building now occupies the site.

# *The Way We Kept Our Cool*

## July 7, 2013

Many modern-day Torontonians are lucky enough to spend their summer holidays at one of the small communities that ring Lake Simcoe or Georgian Bay, in Muskoka or in the Kawarthas. A century or more ago, trips into the hinterland north of the city weren't nearly as popular. Didn't matter, though, those lucky Torontonians had a number of waterfront amusement parks where the cool breezes off Lake Ontario would make the hottest day bearable.

Hanlan's Point Park. Though it's difficult to give a precise date, research indicates that as early as 1870 the sandbar (to be renamed after much landfilling and grooming Hanlan's Point) had the distinction of being the site of the city's earliest amusement park. It all began with a few simple rides that John Hanlan built adjacent to his summer hotel at the west end of Toronto Islands. Incidentally, John is the fellow for whom Hanlan's Point was named, not his more famous son, Ned, the world champion sculler. Over the summers that followed, a larger hotel, more rides, restaurants and games, a dance pavilion and roller rink, and several baseball and lacrosse diamonds were added. For a full description of this fabulous waterfront park read *More Than an Island* by Sally Gibson.

Victoria Park Avenue street sign. Now long gone, one of the city's earliest amusement parks will always be remembered thanks to the name of one of the dusty roads that led to the site on the Lake Ontario shoreline. Victoria Park was a private enterprise started by Peter Patterson, whose Blantyre estate was situated nearby. In addition to a few rides and a small restaurant there were facilities for picnicking and swimming as well as a dance pavilion. And to handle the warm weather crowds a dock was built to accommodate a ferry service to and from the big city to the west. Eventually a streetcar line was extended east out Queen Street, making Victoria Park a true "trolley park," a term that originated south of the border and was used to describe any park served by a trolley line (the term *streetcar* was used locally). The vast majority of these trolley parks were privately owned and in most cases operated by the trolley companies as a way to use their equipment after rush hours and on weekends. Victoria Park operated from 1878 until 1906. Years later the former park became the site of a forest school similar to one operated in High Park. Back then it was felt that children would derive health benefits from being taught in the clean, clear outdoors. The Victoria Park Forest School was closed in the early 1930s to permit the construction of the imposing R.C. Harris Water Treatment Plant, so named to honour the city's Commissioner of Works from 1912 to 1945. Nearby was a much smaller amusement park called Munro Park, so named (though misspelled) for the original property owner, George Monro, a prominent pioneer businessman in both the Town of York and, after 1834, the City of Toronto. Monro served one term (in 1841) as the mayor of Toronto. He died in 1878. Some years after the park closed in 1906 the property was subdivided and houses built, and the street through the new community recognized the old park — though the old chief magistrate's surname name is still misspelled.

Scarboro Beach Park. The main reason both the Victoria and Munro parks closed at the end of the 1906 season was a decision by the Toronto Railway Company (an organization that eventually ran both the older parks and, since 1891, the city's streetcar system as well) to build a larger, more exciting amusement park not far to the west of the Victoria and Munro parks. The new one would cover almost forty acres of what had been the Sisters of St. Joseph's farm, which fronted on a dirt path that was still just an extension of Queen Street. The land ran south to the lake and in today's terms had as its eastern and western boundaries today's Maclean and Leuty avenues. It was on this farm that produce for the Sisters' House of Providence was grown. The new park opened in time for the 1907 season and was served by TRC streetcars, making it another easily accessible trolley park. Complete with a baseball/lacrosse field, a midway, a lookout tower, and a fabulous water slide, this summer place would be called Scarboro Beach Park. It operated until 1925, when it closed and the land was sold off for residential purposes.

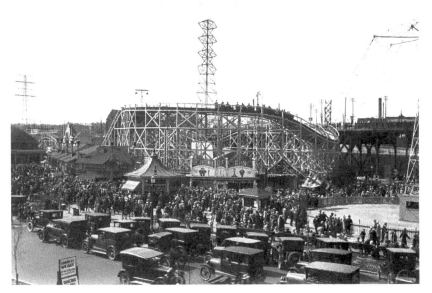

The last of the city's great waterfront amusement parks was Sunnyside. Built in 1922 and operated by the Toronto Harbour Commission (now PortsToronto), the park was located south of the railway tracks at the foot of Roncesvalles Avenue. It had two large merry-go-rounds, a roller coaster, numerous other rides, a selection of games, several restaurants, the always popular Sea Breeze outdoor dance floor, and the converted canoe building factory known as the Palais Royale. The park sat on land reclaimed from the old Humber Bay (as was a long stretch of today's Lake Shore Boulevard West). In 1925 a large swimming pool (known to locals as the tank) was added. The park closed in 1955, killed by the need for better ways for traffic to get in and out of the city. For more about Sunnyside Amusement Park pick up (better still, buy) a copy of my book *I Remember Sunnyside* (Dundurn Press).

# Wonderful Flying Machine

## July 14, 2013

On July 14, 1910, hundreds of Torontonians living in the west end of the city were all abuzz as they tried to explain to many of their neighbours what they had witnessed the night before. It was hard to describe. Many thought it looked like a large bird, but as it moved through the early evening sky the so-called bird's wings didn't flap. In fact, it just seemed to glide southeast towards the harbour. Oh, and there was a strange noise, a kind of buzzing sound. What the heck was it?

It wasn't until that morning's edition of the city's several daily newspapers (remember, no radio, TV, or Internet back then) broke the story that people realized what they had actually seen was a flying machine that had wandered into the city from the air meet being held on mining millionaire William Griffin Trethewey's model farm southeast of the Town of Weston. The "bird" was piloted by Count Jacques Benjamin de Lesseps, a young French aviator and son of Ferdinand de Lesseps, diplomat and creator of the Suez Canal.

De Lesseps and several other like-minded pioneers of the air had accepted an invitation from the fledgling Ontario Motor League to attend a nine-day-long aviation meet that would be presented on the flat plateau of land adjacent to the barns and canning factory just north of the diagonal dirt thoroughfare that connected Keele Street on the east with Jane Street on the west. Originally identified as Holmsted Road, it actually

The Count de Lessep's Blériot monoplane is uncrated upon its arrival by train from an earlier air meet held in Montreal. Its engine and wings were quickly added and the craft was pushed to the nearby airfield on Trethewey's farm, where the count and his Blériot went on to perform a series of flying demonstrations, including the very first flight over our city. (City of Toronto Archives.)

began as a private drive through Trethewey's extensive six-hundred-acre farm property. Following Trethewey's death on March 6, 1926, while wintering in Florida, the officials of the Township of York recognized the millionaire's many and varied philanthropic gestures that benefited the community and they renamed the street Trethewey, as it remains today.

Many flights were undertaken, with most by experienced pilots from Europe and south of the border, the latter preferring the Wright brothers' type of biplane. Once in a while, however, a few like seventeen-year-old Cromwell Dixon, who thought they were pilots, attempted to get their flimsy airplanes off the ground only to suffer embarrassment as their craft skidded into the shrubs and bushes that ringed the field. Fortunately there were no fatalities, just cuts and scrapes. All in all the event was well received by the general public, although as it turned out

The Count Jacques de Lesseps, the first person to fly a heavier-than-air machine over the City of Toronto, a truly "air-raising" event that took place on July 13, 1910. The count died some years later while surveying the barren Quebec forests north of the St. Lawrence River. He is buried in a small cemetery in the community of Gaspé.

there just weren't enough visitors paying the $1 fee, which included admission to the site and the cost of the CPR or Grand Trunk train ride to and from the field, to cover the estimated $35,000 cost of putting on the show.

There's no doubt that the highlight of the meet occurred 103 years ago yesterday when after three circuits of the grass-covered field the Count de Lesseps suddenly pointed his Blériot machine southeast and headed for the big city. Interestingly, this craft was similar to the one in which he had crossed the English Channel a few months earlier, becoming only the second aviator to do so.

The count's epic flight on July 13, 1910, took him out over Hanlan's Point, then in a sweeping curve he turned the craft north up Spadina Avenue to the College Street, intersection, where he turned once again to follow the railway tracks that would lead him and his Blériot back towards Weston and, if his luck and skill held, back to the small airfield that was getting more difficult to see as the day drew to a close.

It was calculated (unofficially, of course, since no one knew what the count had planned — it was something the count himself hadn't planned either) that the daring young man in the flying machine had covered a total of thirty-seven kilometres (his English Channel flight was estimated at thirty-four kilometres), with most of it at a height of a thousand metres, in an elapsed time of thirty-six minutes.

To honour the young aviator's historic flight, William Trethewey presented him with a check for $500 (in Canadian funds, I presume).

The count continued his love affair with flying until one day in the fall of 1927 when he and his mechanic crashed in a dense forest while they were preparing aerial maps of the St. Lawrence River. A memorial to the Count de Lesseps, the first person to fly over our city, can be found in Gaspé, Quebec.

# Never Got Off the Ground

## July 28, 2013

In a previous column I wrote about the proposal put forward back in the late 1950s by four suburban reeves representing York, North York, Etobicoke, and Scarborough suggesting that an above-ground monorail be built along Bloor Street rather than a subway under the thoroughfare. And while that idea was never seriously considered, the four reeves attempted to have staff from the American company that was promoting monorails as a form of rapid transit come to Toronto and convince the skeptical politicians that the concept had merit.

However, while a meeting was eventually arranged, company officials, who sensed growing opposition and had read more than a few derogatory letters to the editor ("Rapid transit is too important to the city than to try and solve the problem with some amusement park ride"), refused to attend or even try to make their case. As a result the Bloor Street monorail never got off the ground (pun intended). The first section of the Bloor-Danforth subway (Keele to Woodbine, or Woodbine to Keele if you're travelling the other direction) opened almost eight years later.

Fifty-plus years ago Bloor Street wasn't the only candidate for a monorail. The ever increasing number of flights into and out of Malton Airport (after 1960 renamed Toronto International Airport and after 1984 Lester B. Pearson International Airport) prompted some to suggest that a high-speed monorail would be the best way to connect

In 1958, while Avro Canada was developing the exciting new Avro Arrow for the RCAF, the company released this sketch of a monorail system that they had proposed as a connecting link between the city's downtown and Malton Airport (now Toronto Pearson). (Photo from the Avro Canada Archives.)

the airfield with downtown Toronto. It could also serve as a commuter line for residents living near its four local stations.

Interestingly, the suggestion came in a June 1958 memo to the Metro Toronto Council from Fred Smye, the executive vice-president of aeronautical projects at A.V. Roe Canada, who had on his list of other things to do the development and, hopefully, full production of the company's revolutionary CF-105 Arrow jet interceptor. It had flown for the first time just a couple of months earlier. (In one of the most contentious decisions ever made by any party in power up in Ottawa, the Arrow project was cancelled on February 20, 1959. More than a half-century later the controversial Lockheed-Martin F-35 may join that club … stay tuned.)

As for the proposed Toronto Union Station–Malton Airport monorail project, the A.V. Roe official suggested elevated trains (operating nine metres over existing railway rights-of-way) could travel up to 120 kilometres per hour and cover the 30-kilometre route in a mere 17 minutes. Stations along the way would include near the Bloor-Dundas intersection (easy access for passengers using the proposed Bloor-Danforth subway), at West Toronto (Dundas-Annette-Dupont), Eglinton (east of Weston Rd.), and in the Town of Weston (north of Lawrence). The trains would curve west over Highways 401 and 27 to a proposed new airport terminal. An extension would feed the Avro aircraft factory and offices as well as the new Woodbine Racetrack that had opened in 1956. The estimated cost of this project was $76 million.

The airport monorail dream ended in September 1958 following its rejection by Metro Toronto's planning commissioner, who cited the report's "unrealistic" costs and (the curse of virtually all public transit projects) competition by the automobile.

Now, more than a half-century later, the idea of a rapid transit connection between Union Station and the airport is back on the rails (another pun intended). The Union Pearson Express, a division of the province's Metrolinx, is under construction, and plans are to have it in service in time for the official opening of the Pan Am and Parapan Am Games on July 10, 2015.

*The Union Pearson Express was officially opened on June 6, 2015.

A postcard view of the original Malton Airport administration building and waiting room. The aircraft were added by an artist to emphasize how, after lagging behind for years, Toronto was quickly becoming a busy aviation hub.

# Never Taxed for a Topic

## August 4, 2013

When some readers find out that I have contributed this column to the Sunday edition of the *Toronto Sun* for more than thirty-five years (and I'm still a teenager, go figure) a few will ask if I have ever been stumped for a subject. After all, submitting a column once a week for thirty-five years equals more than eighteen hundred stories, often with two, sometimes three, historic photos accompanying each. And always with a sincere attempt not to duplicate subjects, although to be honest occasionally newly discovered details will justify a rewrite.

As to whether I have ever come up dry, the simple answer is no. This city and its surrounding communities have so many stories from their respective pasts that the only thing that will get in the way of continuing to tell the Toronto story is the number of gigabytes on my storage device or, dare I say it ... death.

As I was pulling together material for this week's column I suddenly received an email from a reader up in beautiful Orangeville (named not for a colour but for settler Orange Lawrence). Now retired, Steve H. had worked for more than thirty years with the federal income tax people in the stately Dominion Public Building located on the south side of Front Street stretching west from the Yonge Street corner. During all those years, he and his co-workers had been under the impression that 1 Front Street West was one long, imposing building until he came across an old

Looking east along Front Street from near Bay Street, 1931. Note that only the main and easterly parts of Toronto's new Customs Building have been completed. The addition that would extend the stately building west to Bay Street wouldn't be completed for another four years.

photo that showed that when built it was much shorter, stretching only about half the block. "What's the story?" Steve asked in his note. After looking at the old picture I too was intrigued, and my original subject for today was quickly relegated to a back burner.

Quite frankly, I knew very little about the building even though for many years, to save the postage, I would deposit the envelope with my income tax forms (and the required cheque) in the drop box outside the main entrance. At that time I was in no mood to stand around and study the building.

Now, however, Steve's request piqued my interest. When it comes to history, not knowing the answer to a question and searching for it is always better than having the answer right off the bat.

I began by researching Toronto's Dominion Public Building, and I came up with nothing. That's because the structure was built as the city's new Customs House. Once I latched on to the correct title I found lots of interesting material. For instance, while the city had been requesting the Dominion government to replace the old, small, and badly outdated Customs House since 1913, a world war broke out, putting any non-military government spending out of the question.

Sixteen years would pass before the Customs House project was revived (and you think the Scarborough extension project has taken a long time to get off, or under, the ground?). The first photos and plans of the project on the south side of Front Street west of Yonge appeared in the newspapers in mid-February 1928. The $2.1-million contract was awarded to the Peter Lyall Construction Co. in early July of the following year, and excavation on a site still covered in many places by the ruins of the Great Toronto Fire of 1904 began at the end of 1929. By August 1, 1931, all of the customs and tax collecting offices that had been scattered across downtown Toronto were relocated in the partially completed building.

As for why Steve saw a photo of the building in a half-completed state, it was because of more money problems, this time brought on by the Great Depression. Money was again tight, and combined with diminishing income and customs payments from troubled businesses, the government decided to postpone completing the $546,000 addition west to the Bay Street corner until better times returned. The building was finally completed in the spring of 1935.

# Scarborough's Lost Dream

## August 18, 2013

The transit riding public must shake their heads when attempts to improve service get derailed (pun intended) by elected officials who may mean well but who, for reasons that usually have nothing to do with the facts, confuse and confound so that eventually nothing gets done. A good case in point is what to do with the Bloor-Danforth subway extension into Scarborough. Is it to be simply an extension of the present line from Kennedy Station to the Scarborough Town Centre, or will it be the Metrolinx light rail proposal? One version doesn't have the funds, the other the approval of City Council. I've even asked a few elected officials, and if the truth be known even they don't seem to know what will happen next.

Now let me take you back forty-four years to the day in September 1969 when a report was put forward by members of the TTC planning staff, known worldwide for their expertise in moving people by public transit. That report recommended that the eastern terminal of the Bloor-Danforth subway at Warden Station be extended via a private right-of-way that utilized a little-used railway spur line and Hydro right-of-way to connect with not just the planned Scarborough Town Centre (which opened in May 1973) but also the proposed Malvern housing development and, eventually, east to a new zoo at Glen Rouge, which would one day (August 15, 1974) replace the old Riverdale Zoo in downtown Toronto.

On a bright, sunny September 17, 1963, transit historian John Bromley took this photo of a multiple-unit train consisting of two PCC streetcars (the following vehicle purchased used from the City of Cleveland a decade earlier) heading west on the Danforth at Pape Avenue. A proposal put forward by the TTC in 1969 would have seen trains such as this one operating on the Bloor-Danforth subway extension carrying passengers to and from the farthest reaches of what was then still the Borough of Scarborough. On the north side of the Danforth (almost always "the" Danforth, not Danforth Avenue) just east of the intersection is the Palace Theatre that opened in 1924 and closed in 1987 after entertaining neighbourhood moviegoers for sixty-three years.

It was also recommended that the vehicles dedicated to this proposed line be the Commission's 175 or so surplus PCC streetcars, some of which had been removed from the Bloor-Danforth streetcar line when the new subway opened from Islington to Warden in 1968 (Kipling to Kennedy opened a dozen years later). In rush hour these PCCs could be joined together in "trains" of up to seven cars.

As an aside, this same report featured a thirty-five-mile-long rapid transit line that would encircle the city, connecting with the Yonge and Spadina subway lines and incorporating spur lines that would connect with Toronto Pearson International Airport and Woodbine Racetrack.

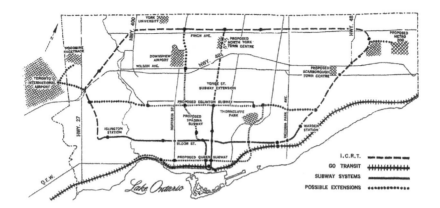

This map appeared in the September 18, 1969, newspapers and outlined the massive public transit plan the TTC visualized. The project would start with a high-speed streetcar line that would connect the Warden Station on the Bloor-Danforth subway with the proposed Scarborough Town Centre, the Malvern housing development, and the new zoo in the Rouge River Valley.

Wow! Imagine if this plan had been implemented. Today we wouldn't be arguing about the Bloor-Danforth subway … oops, LRT … oops, subway extension into Scarborough.

# Getting There from Here

## August 25, 2013

In a recent column I related the ongoing saga of how the easterly extension of the Bloor-Danforth subway could have been solved decades ago if the TTC's 1969 plan to use "trains" consisting of up to seven or eight tried and true PCC streetcars operating on off-street private rights-of-way had been followed. This week I'm featuring a good news story that describes how politicians came up with a plan to assist drivers settle the age-old problem of getting there from here, the "there" being Scarborough, the "here" being the city, or vice versa.

Prior to the summer of 1957, the only way to get to Scarborough from the city (or to the city from Scarborough) was to use a meandering route through north Toronto, Leaside, and East York. Immediately following the creation of the Municipality of Metropolitan Toronto in 1953 (which came into being January 1 of the following year) planning began to improve the flow of traffic across Metro, which even back then was causing serious problems.

Plans for a new lakeshore expressway, Don Valley Parkway, and something called the Spadina arterial highway were all on the drawing boards. And there was one more, the Eglinton Crosstown highway, soon to be known simply as the Eglinton Avenue East Extension. The total cost of these four projects was $150 million.

The first of the four to be completed was the Eglinton Extension, which connected Leaside on the west with Scarborough on the east, a

$4.25-million project that took three years to complete, a full six months ahead of schedule. It was officially opened on August 26, 1957 by Ontario Premier Leslie Frost, accompanied by Metro Chairman Fred Gardiner and former Toronto city mayor Alan Lamport. It was predicted the new route would decrease the travel time between Leaside and Scarborough from sixteen minutes (via O'Connor Drive, etc.) to just six minutes.

The first rush hour after the opening, there was traffic chaos with cars and trucks backed up for miles.

How does the saying go ... build it and they will come.

This photo was taken in 1956. It shows the west end of the new Eglinton Avenue East Extension at the intersection of Eglinton Avenue East and Brentcliffe Road in Leaside. The signs warn drivers headed east to Scarborough that they would have to find another route, at least until August 26, 1957, when the new road would be officially opened. For many that other route was via St. Clair, Mount Pleasant, Moore, Southvale, Millwood, Donlands, and O'Connor Drive. (Photo from the City of Toronto Archives.)

This 1956 aerial view shows the east end of the soon-to-be-opened Eglinton Extension at its new intersection with Victoria Park Avenue. The view looks northwest, with O'Connor Drive running across the bottom where it crosses Victoria Park and connects with the existing Eglinton Avenue East. The legendary Golden Mile Plaza, built at a cost of $4 million and officially opened on April 8, 1954, is at the northeast corner of Eglinton and Victoria Park avenues. It was home to Zellers, Hunt's Bakery, Liggett's drugstore, and the largest supermarket in Canada, Loblaws, which was visited by Queen Elizabeth II during her Toronto visit in 1959. Eglinton Square is at the bottom of the view, where there was a Dominion store (now Metro) and a huge Aikenhead's hardware store. (Photo courtesy Rick Schofield, Scarborough Archives.)

# City Joined the Streetcar Biz

## September 8, 2013

Things were so much easier one hundred years ago, especially when it came to moving people from A to B and back again. For instance, as the second decade of the twentieth century approached, the population of Toronto was increasing rapidly, almost doubling from nearly 200,000 in 1900 to more than 350,000 in 1911. There were similar increases in the outlying suburban areas over that same time period.

Unfortunately, what wasn't increasing were initiatives to improve the ability of the existing public transportation to handle the ever increasing crowds making their way from the outlying residential areas to the downtown business and shopping districts. From a business standpoint this decision was understandable since the streetcars back then were operated by the Toronto Railway Company, a private company. As long as there were insufficient numbers of passengers to justify buying additional vehicles and spending money to lay track and string overhead wire into the scarcely populated areas outside the city boundaries (as they were when the TRC was granted its monopoly in 1891) the company management refused to improve the suburban service. After all, profits came first.

But something had to be done. City officials initially asked the directors to expand the system, and when they were turned down city lawyers tried to get the Privy Council in England to order the TRC to comply with the city's request. No luck there either. The situation was getting desperate.

In 1916, commuters, who have just arrived from downtown on a Toronto Railway Company Avenue Road streetcar, wait to board streetcars operating on the Toronto Civic Railways' St. Clair route. Adult fares were 2¢, tickets six for a dime. Then on November 1, 1921, two months after the creation of the new city-operated TTC, these two routes became part of the TTC with tracks and switches finally laid to connect both. The historic Timothy Eaton Memorial Church on the north side of St. Clair Avenue West, between Dunvegan Road and Warren Road, can be seen in the background of both photos.

In 1911 the city came up with a solution: it would establish its own street railway venture, to be known as the Toronto Civic Railways and to operate as part of the city's Works Department. The TCR would build and operate five lines completely separate from the private city system.

Commuters could soon access downtown on new routes laid out along Bloor Street West (from Dundas Street West to Runnymede Road), on the Danforth (from Broadview east to Luttrell Avenue), on Lansdowne Avenue (from St. Clair Avenue to the CPR crossing north of Dupont Street), on Gerrard Street (from Greenwood Avenue to Main Street) and on St. Clair Avenue West (from Yonge Street west to the Grand Trunk Railway crossing west of Caledonia Avenue). All five lines were opened (much to the relief of the commuting public) between 1912 (Gerrard) and 1917 (Lansdowne). All were absorbed by the newly created TTC on September 1, 1921.

Interestingly, both the Gerrard and St. Clair routes continue to be served by streetcars, the former by vehicles on the 506 Carlton line and the latter by the 512 St. Clair cars, a route that to be sure has had its foes and allies.

This view also looks west on St. Clair Avenue towards Avenue Road, but ninety-seven years later. (Photo courtesy Yarmila Filey.)

# Toronto's Union Station, Then and Then

## September 15, 2013

As work continues (seemingly forever) on upgrades to Toronto's magnificent Union Station, here's a look at stations that held that same title in the city's past. Incidentally, to be allocated the name Union Station the facility must serve at least two railway companies.

Built in 1871–72 to replace the city's first Union Station (basically just a couple of wooden sheds south of the present Front and Bay intersection that had opened coincident with the arrival of the first passenger trains in 1858), Toronto's second Union Station is seen here in this circa 1880 photo. It was located between Front Street and Toronto Bay just west of York Street. In modern terms it would have been about where the Skywalk to the Dome is today. Built in 1871–72, this station was described as "the most beautiful on the continent" and was officially opened on July 1, 1873. Note the station had three through tracks with waiting rooms nearby and offices located in the three towers. During the construction of the station a large clock with four faces was installed in the middle tower. That clock is still telling time, but not here in Toronto.

As passenger traffic in and out of the old Union Station increased, railway officials decided to enlarge the station by building an addition to the north. The new seven-storey office building fronted on the south side of Front Street opposite the foot of today's University Avenue. In the background of this 1909 postcard view, which shows the 1895 addition, the main tower of the old station is visible, as is its clock.

Even with the 1895 addition, Toronto's Union Station was bursting at the seams. And while a modern new station had been sought for decades, it wasn't until land on the south side of Front Street between Bay and York streets was cleared of ruined buildings following the huge fire of 1904 that one became available. Still, it wasn't until 1913 that work on today's present station actually began. However, nearly two decades would pass before the new (and present) Union Station was in full operation. In the meantime, as seen in this July 1927 photo, crews are removing the old station's train sheds. Next came the job of getting rid of the trio of towers. But they were so well built that the job would take another six months. Before demolition of the central tower began, crews removed the clock and its mechanism. The clock face can just be seen through the smoke near the top of the tower to the left of the photo. Soon this historic timepiece would be on its way north to its new home in Huntsville.

In late August 1927, Charles Paget, chairman of the Town of Huntsville's Parks Commission, presented his hometown with the clock from Toronto's second Union Station. And just where is it? Well, if you're going to the Cranberry Festival in Bala this October why not visit nearby Huntsville, where you can inspect and set your watch to the clock in its town hall tower. That timepiece is the one that told Torontonians the time from 1872 until 1927 from its place in the tower of our second Union Station.

# Toronto's Worst Disaster

## September 22, 2013

Sixty-four years seems like a long time ago, but for those who were living anywhere in Canada in the fall of 1949, a fire on board a Great Lakes cruise ship berthed alongside Toronto Harbour's Pier 9 will never be forgotten. And for those who weren't yet born, suffice it to say that the burning of the SS *Noronic* has (and here's the good news) remained the worst disaster, of any kind, to befall our city.

Fire officials eventually determined that the conflagration was the result of a small fire of undetermined origin that had erupted in the port side linen closet on "C" deck early in the morning of September 17, 1949. This occurrence, which was to doom the ship and 118 of her 524 passengers, began less than eight hours after the ship arrived in port. Only one of the *Noronic*'s 171-member crew and, as it turned out the only Canadian victim (all the other victims were American citizens) was Louisa Dustin of Sarnia who succumbed to her injuries a little more than three weeks after the fire.

The ship's departure from Toronto was scheduled for 7:00 p.m. on the evening of the 17th with her destination being Prescott, Ontario. A sightseeing cruise of the 1000 Islands would follow with a return trip to Detroit, where the trip had originated, arriving there early in the morning of September 21.

The rest of the pleasure trip would never happen. In fact, the last trip the fire-ravaged ship would make was to the wrecker's yard next to the Steel Company of Canada's sprawling factory in Hamilton.

As the wreck was towed out of Toronto Harbour, medical personnel were faced with the incredibly difficult task of identifying *Noronic*'s 118 victims. DNA methods so common today were years in the future, and X-rays could do little to identify what were nothing more than piles of charred remains. Nevertheless, officials were able to confirm the identity of all but thirteen victims. Since that sad day so many years ago, the unclaimed remains have rested in a grave in Mount Pleasant Cemetery.

Passengers line the railings of the iconic Great Lakes cruise ship SS *Noronic* as she makes her way through one of the locks at Sault Ste. Marie. Close inspection of the undated photo reveals several uniformed soldiers guarding the canal, indicating the picture may have been taken sometime during the years of the Great War when sabotage was a serious concern. Note also the names "Northern Navigation Co." and "Grand Trunk Ry. Line" painted on the side of the ship. The first was the company that commissioned the construction of *Noronic* by a Port Arthur (now part of Thunder Bay) shipyard in 1913, while the second name accentuated the fact that the ship's owner, the Canada Steamship Line, used a combination of ship and rail to transport thousands of immigrants (and others) to the wide open country that was western Canada.

As a result of tons of water being poured on the flaming ship, SS *Noronic* eventually sank to the bottom at Pier 9, which was located just east of the foot of Yonge Street. According to Toronto waterfront historian Jay Bascom, the ship's location in today's terms would have been somewhere in the middle of the Westin Harbour Castle hotel's lobby. In this photo taken the day after the September 17, 1949, disaster, two people examine the scarred ship while in the background water continues to be poured on a still smoldering area of the ill-fated vessel.

# Can't Beat New City Hall

## September 29, 2013

Although we still call it New City Hall, in actual fact this iconic building just turned forty-eight years old. Though hardly new, the structure will continue to retain that modifier as long as we have our Old City Hall just across Bay Street. As some will recall, we would have lost this precious landmark back in 1967 had City Council not rejected a request from department store magnate John David Eaton that would have seen his company purchase the land on which the 1899 building stood. Such a purchase would have quickly resulted in Old City Hall's demolition along with the removal of two other nearby historic structures, the 1847 Church of the Holy Trinity and the Rev. Henry Scadding's 1857 residence.

With the Eaton's deal dead, the city embarked on a major restoration project that saw one of Toronto's few remaining landmark buildings given a new lease on life as a provincial courthouse. And who knows, perhaps one day it'll be home to a The Story of Toronto civic museum. Stranger things have happened.

Interestingly, just as plans for the future of the old building were mired in controversy, so too were the plans and the drawings and the models of the proposed new civic building that would replace it on a site on the west side of Bay Street.

Acting on Mayor Nathan Phillips's suggestion, City Council agreed to hold an international competition to select the design for Toronto's new

Site clearing is underway in this April 1962 photo looking down on the site of Toronto's New City Hall. The parking lot under what would become Nathan Phillips Square was already open when the *Toronto Telegram* newspaper photographer snapped (we don't "snap" pictures anymore) this fascinating image. To the left of the municipal building's unique footprint is the old Registry Building, and while a suggestion was made that it be relocated somewhere "out of the way," it was ultimately demolished. Note on the skyline to the right of centre is the tallest building in the city based on its height above sea level. Located on St. Clair Avenue West between Yonge and Avenue Road, this building opened as the head office of Imperial Oil. It was recently repurposed as the Imperial Lofts condominium. To the right of the photo is Bay Street and to the north at the Bay and Dundas corner is the infamous Ford Hotel (and no, it has no connection with today's chief magistrate).

city hall. In total, 520 concepts were submitted, and from those the judges selected eight finalists. That number was soon narrowed down to one, that being the design submitted by Finnish architect Viljo Revell. It was when that decision was announced on September 26, 1958, that the controversy erupted. Many Torontonians thought the design was, in a word, "awful," while others were concerned that the cost of the new building would exceed the $18-million projected cost. (By the time the new city hall opened on September 13, 1965, that figure had almost doubled to $31 million).

However, the most scathing comments about Revell's creation came from world-renowned architect Frank Lloyd Wright during an interview with Pierre Berton soon after the design was made public. In Wright's

Finnish architect Viljo Revell's striking New City Hall is pictured through the ruins of the legendary Casino Theatre on the south side of Queen Street just two months before its official opening. Incidentally, a similar view today would be blocked by the Sheraton Centre.

Viljo Revell, the architect of Toronto's New City Hall. He died less than a year before his creation was officially opened.

opinion, the Finnish architect's design was "a piece of categorical sterility." And what's worse, he continued, by accepting the competition winner "Toronto will have a headmarker for a grave and future generations will look at it and say it marks the spot where Toronto fell."

Revell replied to the criticism, saying, "Mr. Wright is the greatest architect we have. He has taught many, many things to younger architects like myself. He is a great man."

In a strange coincidence, both Wright and Revell died before they had a chance to see the completed New City Hall, the former in 1959, the latter in 1964.

# When Vaudeville Ruled

**October 6, 2013**

Nestled in amongst all the new high rise office and condominium towers in the very heart of downtown Toronto is a remarkable pair of theatrical gems all wrapped up in one elegant hundred-year-old structure.

Built and opened in late 1913, American motion picture executive and pioneer motion picture theatre owner Marcus Loew's new high-class vaudeville house would also feature photoplays (silent movies), which were still very much the entertainment marvel of the age. The huge playhouse was Loew's first Canadian venture and would soon become the flagship of his chain of Canadian theatres. After looking at and rejecting a site at the southwest corner of Richmond and Victoria streets, Loew decided on locating on the east side of Yonge Street just north of the busy Queen Street intersection. No doubt the idea of hordes of potential customers looking for a break in their exhausting day of shopping in the nearby Robert Simpson and T. Eaton department stores helped Loew make up his mind.

And if this huge new theatre wasn't enough excitement for the local theatre-going public, less than two months later Loew opened the magical Winter Garden high atop the Yonge Street theatre.

When vaudeville "died," the main floor theatre switched to "talkies" and for a variety of reasons the Winter Garden was simply closed up tight.

This photo was taken in the late summer of 1929, just weeks before the Great Depression took the shine off an otherwise busy city. We are looking south on Yonge Street from just north of Queen Street. To the extreme left of the photo is the former 1903 Heintzman Hall, which still stands. Next to it is the hundred-year-old Loews Yonge Street Theatre, and next to it is Diana's Tea Room. Over the years this establishment grew to become one of the city's most popular family restaurants. Across the street from these three businesses were Woolworth's 5¢ and 10¢ emporium and the Eaton's and John Northway's department stores.

Featured in this April 1920 ad for the Loews and Winter Garden are several vaudeville acts, a photoplay (silent movie), and what was called a "chaser," usually something that was so bad that it would chase people out of the theatre so a new crop of cash customers could be seated. Of special interest in the ad are the names Stan and Mae Laurel. Yes, that's the same Stan Laurel who seven years later would team up with Oliver Hardy to become Laurel and Hardy, arguably the world's funniest comedy team. As shown in this newspaper ad, Stan's stage partner was the former Mae Dahlberg, an Australian comedienne who, it is recorded, gave her partner, the former Arthur Stanley Jefferson, a new surname, Laurel. Though the pair was never legally married she carried his name until they separated in 1925. It was about the same time that Stan left the stage for films, where in 1927 he teamed up with "Ollie" in the pair's first movie *Duck Soup* (and no, not the better known Marx Brothers feature of the same name).

As the years passed, the 1913 theatre began to lose its charm. In fact, with mounting development pressures all around it the theatre's final days appeared numbered.

Then to the rescue came the Ontario Heritage Foundation (now the Ontario Heritage Trust), and after a 2.5-year, $30-million restoration program in 1989 the world's only "double-deck" theatre complex was back in business, but as the renamed Elgin and Winter Garden Theatre Centre. In addition to the two historic theatres, the Centre features new rehearsal studios, loading docks, and additional lounges and in its new life has become home to numerous live theatre performances, special events, award presentations, film screenings, and corporate events.

# Take the Time to Go to Jail

## October 20, 2013

Recently, Corrections Canada ordered the closing of the Kingston Penitentiary. But before the place was made off limits to the curious it was decided to offer tours to the general public, with all the money raised from admission fees donated to the United Way of Kingston. Our friends and now residents of Kingston (the city, not the pen) Joy and Dave Garrick invited us to visit with them and together we would tour the 1835 structure. But wouldn't you know it, before Dave could even order tickets the nearly ten thousand that were made available were scooped up. So much for going to jail.

It seems that as bad as such places of incarceration (and the things that happen therein) may be, jails and penitentiaries hold a fascination for many people. On the few occasions during the city's Doors Open weekends when the old Don Jail held an open house the crowds were immense, with the place holding the record for number of visitors.

The Don began welcoming its first few visitors in 1864, an opening that was delayed when fire almost destroyed the building while it was still under construction. This event must have upset the jail's architect, William Thomas, who had only recently celebrated the opening of his new St. Lawrence Hall down on King Street.

It wasn't long after the Don Jail took in its first "guests" that people began complaining that it was unhealthy, overcrowded, and

In the foreground of this souvenir penny postcard we see the "softly flowing" Don River just north of the Gerrard Street bridge. On the hill overlooking the river is the city's Smallpox Hospital that was built in 1872 on the site of the House of Refuge. The Smallpox Hospital was where victims of this awful scourge, one that ravaged the city on several occasions, were treated. To the extreme right of the view is a portion of the infamous Don Jail. Faced with demolition on several occasions, its rotunda and several jail cells have recently been incorporated in the new Bridgepoint Hospital.

had numerous other shortfalls. In fact, in 1915 Toronto mayor Tommy Church announced that jail would soon be closed, with all the inmates, male and female (yes, there was a time when the Don Jail was home to both men and women), sent to the new Industrial Farm a few miles east of Yonge Street and south of Richmond Hill.

While numerous attempts were made to close the place, that actually didn't happen until 1977. In the intervening 113 years a total of 70 inmates met their fate at the end of a rope. That number included Arthur Lucas and Ronald Turpin, who, on December 11, 1962, became the last two people to be executed in Canada. Two other notables were Steve Suchan and Michael Jackson, members of the notorious Boyd Gang who were hanged at the Don for the killing of Sergeant of Detectives Edmond Tong, a twenty-three-year veteran of the Toronto police force.

When a few people took ceremonial swings at the ornate entranceway to the jail on December 31, 1977, others waited to see if there wasn't some way to preserve at least portions of a building that had become a sad but important part of Toronto's past. One such person was Mayor

Not far from the site of those early smallpox and isolation hospitals stands the striking new Bridgepoint Active Healthcare building, which opened its doors earlier this year. In the background is the shell of the 1963 "half-round" Riverdale Hospital, presently in the process of being demolished. To the right of the view is the repurposed Don Jail, and to the east of it is the Toronto Jail that is still very much in business.

While major areas of the old Don Jail have been transformed into administrative and conference facilities for the staff at Bridgepoint, the main entrance, rotunda, and several of the jail cells have been retained. In these two photos we see the rotunda and four of the original cells.

David Crombie, who reserved judgment on the jail's demolition until all preservation avenues had been explored.

It took some time, but when the decision was eventually made to replace the nearby Riverdale convalescent hospital with a new facility, to be known as Bridgepoint (at the eastern point of the Gerrard bridge), it was agreed that portions of the old jail would serve the administrative needs of the new hospital.

Next time you're in the Gerrard and Broadview neighbourhood take a few moments and go to jail.

# Pachyderms from the Past

## October 27, 2013

Now that the dust has settled, both figuratively and physically, and Toka, Iringa, and Thika have arrived at their new home in the Performing Animals Welfare Society sanctuary near San Andreas, California, it gives me a chance to write about just a few of the many elephants that have entertained Torontonians.

The first elephants seen by any Torontonian were those that city politician, businessman, and entrepreneur Harry Piper had on display in his Wild Animal Zoo, located at the northeast corner of Front and York streets. Little is known about the history of this attraction other than it was operated by the Zoological and Acclimatization Society and opened to the public in the early 1880s. We don't even know how long it operated except that a story about a hurricane that swept through Toronto in 1895 mentioned that the billboards that surrounded the site of Piper's zoo had been blown over by the strong wind. Even less is known about the elephants, and the only real evidence we have that they even existed can be found in a sketch that accompanies this column and was drawn from memory by a resident of the city for an early newspaper story. By the way, it was the whale from Piper's zoo (which was actually the carcass of a dead whale found near the Gaspé and brought to the Toronto zoo as an interesting, albeit often smelly, exhibit each summer) that resulted in a mystery many years later. That mystery came about when the tunnel

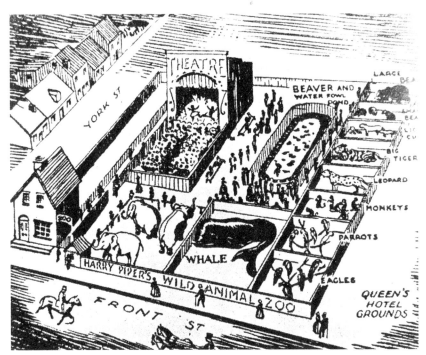

An artist's circa 1890 sketch shows the layout of Harry Piper's Wild Animal Zoo, a city attraction that came complete with lions and tigers and bears and more, oh my. Plus a poor dead whale whose buried remains were to result in an interesting mystery nearly a century later. The zoo was located next door to the province's pre-eminent hotel, the Queen's, and opposite the future site of today's Union Station. The attraction's flamboyant owner is remembered to this day in the name of the small street behind the Royal York as well as in the name of the pub located on the hotel's lower level.

for the new Harbourfront streetcar line under Bay Street south of Front was being dug. One day workers found what was identified as a piece of whale vertebrae, something that stunned experts since no salt water mammals were known to have ever existed in this area. A quick search of the history books and I was able to convince those experts that the mystery bone was actually all that remained of Piper's whale, which was disposed of in the bay across from the zoo and subsequently buried during the ongoing reclamation of the city's waterfront.

The next pachyderm we know about is the one presented to the city's zoo, which had been established in 1894 in Riverdale Park at the instigation of another city politician, businessman, and entrepreneur with an absolutely perfect surname, Daniel Lamb. This elephant, known

THE GLOBE. TORONTO. SATURDAY,. JULY 8, 1882—TWELVE-PAGE SHEET.

Amusements.

## RYAN & ROBINSON'S
# Mammoth Circus and Menagerie !
Three Times Larger Than Ever, and Positively the Best in the World, will Exhibit in
## TORONTO, FRIDAY AND SATURDAY, JULY 14 and 15,
Giving Two Grand, Full, and Complete Performances Each Day, Afternoon and Night, at popular prices, under the personal direction of the great
# JAMES ROBINSON,
the champion bareback rider of the world, who will make his second and last appearance before a Dominion audience prior to his departure for Europe at the close of the present season. What those who visit this Mammoth Combination will see :—
## A GROUP OF AFRICAN ELEPHANTS, INCLUDING ROMEO, THE WAR ELEPHANT.

You want elephants? A full-page ad in the July 8, 1882, edition of The Globe newspaper announced that Ryan and Robinson's Mammoth Circus and Menagerie would be presented the following Friday and Saturday on the vacant lot at the northeast corner of King and Portland streets. The event would feature "a group of African elephants, including Romeo, the war elephant" (the ad didn't reveal what Romeo had done to have been thusly described). In addition, "twin jumbo baby elephants valued at $30,000" would be presented, and they would also participate in "a gorgeous free street pageant."

as Sir John, was presented to the zoo in 1902 by the Toronto Railway Company, the city's privately owned street railway enterprise that was replaced by our present TTC in 1921. Turns out there was an ulterior motive for the officials donating the gift. The number of paying passengers travelling to the zoo on the company streetcars especially to see Sir John increased dramatically.

As a kid, I used to visit the old zoo with my parents and brother Bob, but I couldn't remember seeing any elephants. Thanks to long-time friend and Cabbagetown historian George Rust-D'Eye, I was able to confirm that as kids we in fact did see elephants at the old zoo before it closed its doors in the summer of 1974. But neither of us was sure whether any of the Riverdale elephants went to the new zoo in Scarborough later that summer. Anyone know?

And of course there were elephants that appeared at the various circuses held over the years at Maple Leaf Gardens and under makeshift tents erected on some of the city's larger parking lots. And I recall going with my parents to the famous Clyde Brothers Circus held at the old Maple Leaf baseball stadium at the foot of Bathurst Street.

# Our First Remembrance

## November 10, 2013

When Torontonians finally received the news that the so-called war to end all wars had finally ended, it wasn't long before thousands of them took to the streets to celebrate both joy and relief. Officially the armistice was to come into effect at the eleventh hour on the eleventh day of the eleventh month of 1918. To be historically accurate, the treaty had actually been signed six hours earlier (at 5:00 a.m. French time) with an agreement that the document was to become effective at 11:00 a.m. that same morning.

Interestingly, so eager were some people to get that miserable war over that when the travelling message board in the front window of one of the local papers broke the news that the war had ended on November 7, 1918, no questions were asked and no confirmations sought. It was time to party. As a result, some parts of the city were busy celebrating while other areas were still anticipating some official notification.

The Associated Press, the organization that reported the end of the war prematurely, rescinded the report. Festivities would have to wait another few days until official confirmation was received.

But November 11, 1918, would be the last time the end of the war would be celebrated. As people began to realize the enormous human consequences of the four-year war, festivities turned to sadness. The first anniversary of the end of the war to end all wars, the one that began

During their cross-Canada tour in 1939 King George VI and Queen Elizabeth paid a one-day visit to Toronto. After meeting with civic officials at the City Hall (Mayor Ralph Day and Mrs. Day can be seen behind the royal couple) the king and queen were met by many of their loyal citizens at several huge events held in locations around Toronto. As they left city hall they passed by the cenotaph and one wonders if they remarked on its similarity to the much larger Great Cenotaph in Whitehall, London, England.

Anne de Haas took this poignant photograph of Toronto Police Constable Harold Williamson and his mount Juno Beach attending Remembrance Day services at the cenotaph in Kew Gardens.

The city's new cenotaph was photographed soon after it was dedicated on November 11, 1925. In the background, a pair of TTC Peter Witt streetcars can be seen operating on Queen Street. (Photo from the City of Toronto Archives.)

in early August 1914 and was certain to be over by Christmas of that same year, became a day to remember and honour those who would never return. On that day, November 11, 1919, Torontonians gathered in front of City Hall (now Old City Hall) and placed hundreds of wreaths of remembrance around a makeshift wooden cross. It wasn't until well after the Remembrance Day service of 1923 that Toronto City Council agreed that a proper cenotaph (from the Greek *kenotaphion,* a term meaning "empty tomb") should be erected. Some said it took longer to make that decision than it did to fight the war.

Nevertheless, $25,000 was set aside for a proper memorial. After designs were sought, one submitted by local architects Thomas Pomphrey and William Ferguson was selected, and work on the new cenotaph began. On July 24, 1924, the cornerstone was tapped into place by Field Marshal Douglas Haig, the 1st Earl Haig, commander of the British Expeditionary Force. The following year, on November 11, 1925, Toronto's new cenotaph, fashioned out of granite from the Canadian Shield, was dedicated by Governor General Sir Julian Byng, 1st Baron Byng of Vimy.

Lest We Forget.

# First TTC Rider Paid 7¢ Fare

## November 17, 2013

On September 1, 1921, the first person to use the services of the new Toronto Transportation Commission deposited his 7¢ in the fare box. Little did he or any of the city's 522,000 or so citizens realize that this gentleman would be the first of more than more than 29 billion people who would, over the next ninety-two years, use a system that we now know simply as the good old TTC (the term *Transportation* was replaced with the word *Transit* co-incident with the opening of the Yonge subway in 1954).

One thing that he would have known when he boarded the streetcar on King Street was that this was the same type of vehicle he had ridden just the previous day. Why was he paying a fare that was 40 percent higher than the nickel he had deposited in that same fare box just one day earlier?

The answer was simple. It was a new company that was operating the city's transportation services. It had taken over operations from the privately owned Toronto Railway Company, which had had its way from 1891 until August 30, 1921. The new TTC had inherited a rundown and inefficient transit operation that needed a lot of upgrading, both in terms of equipment and (to use a word that's heard a lot these days) infrastructure.

In the beginning, the backbone of the service fleet consisted of hundreds of streetcars of various types. There were just a few buses (double-deckers with open tops ... not so great in the winter or on routes with low

A rare photo of the half-mile racetrack that was built in 1912 by the Hillcrest Driving Club on part of the large MacNamara farm located at the southwest corner of Bathurst Street and Davenport Road. A small market garden was established on the inner portion of the track. The president of the Driving Club was Sam McBride, who served as Toronto's mayor on two occasions.

bridges) on the TTC's roster. And while subways (referred to as "tubes" back then) had been discussed, they were still decades in the future.

Streetcar repairs and modernization had taken place in a number of buildings in and around the Front and Sherbourne streets intersection, with most of those structures dating back to the horse car days of the 1880s. It was decided to bring all the streetcar repair locations together, and to accomplish that goal most of the former Hillcrest racetrack and part of what was left of the adjacent farm were purchased by the TTC. This location was chosen since it was deemed close to the geographical centre of the city (as it then was) and near the centre of the street railway network the TTC was planning to set up. After more than three years of design and construction work the first buildings of the new Hillcrest complex opened in 1925. Then came the ordering of new streetcars, the large Peter Witts and trailers, and most of the trackwork and overhead as well as the various electrical substations had to be repaired or replaced. Safety and efficiency were now paramount.

Of course, all these projects cost money, and lots of it. And that's why Mr. Smith (unfortunately, there's no record of passenger #1's real name) had to add those two pennies to that old 5¢ fare.

Many disgruntled passengers thought they'd get back at the TTC and its bosses by throwing seven pennies in the fare box. Sorting, counting, and wrapping those thousands of coins got to be a real pain.

# Mi Casa Es Su Casa

## November 24, 2013

It was the late fall of 1912 when Mr. and Mrs. Henry Pellatt moved into their brand new house on the hill north of the winding, dirt-covered Davenport Road on the northwestern outskirts of Toronto. After living at several different city addresses, the couple were pretty sure this would be the place they could spend the rest of their lives.

After all, Henry was one of the nation's richest money barons; though he was financially well off, all the invoices accumulated during the lengthy construction of his new residence were not yet in.

On the other hand, money was a real concern for the castle's architect, Edward James Lennox. He was still trying to get all the money he was owed by the city for his work designing and ultimately supervising the construction of the new City Hall at the top of Bay Street. His work had been completed with the opening of his magnificent creation in the fall of 1899, yet Lennox was still waiting for a good chunk of the money owing.

After only about a decade in their new home, the Pellatts soon began to wonder whether they could continue to afford the ever-increasing cost of the hundreds of tons of coal to heat the barn of a place. That expense combined with other costs and a seemingly never-ending reassessment of the castle, the stables, and the property by city tax officials.

Eventually it all became too much, and in the early 1920s they moved out, taking up residence in their Lake Mary residence near King City.

Talented craftsmen take a few minutes to pose for the photographer as the new one-hundred-room residence with at least five thousand electric lights being built for Canadian multi-millionaire Sir Henry Pellatt takes shape behind them. Built on the escarpment that once formed the shoreline of a prehistoric lake, the one-of-a-kind Mansion Well's Hill (which, according to Carlie Oreskovich, author of *The King of the Castle*, is the unique structure's original name) was the best way Sir Henry could one-up his fellow businessmen who were forced to live in houses that had only ten or twenty rooms and half a dozen of those newfangled electric lights, though it's more than likely those rooms were still lit by gas.

To try and cover costs that were out of control thanks to bad investments and a worsening business climate, Pellatt decided to offer the castle for sale. It looked for a time like the federal government would purchase the castle for a much needed military hospital.

At the same time, Toronto-born motion picture star (the first person to be given that title) Mary Pickford suggested the place could be her summer home away from the hustle and bustle of Hollywood. Then there was the high school that was so badly needed by the families in the fast growing nearby neighbourhood.

But the thing that looked most promising was a luxury apartment house that was proposed in late 1925 by an American enterprise, the Fuller Construction Co. They would add extensions to the east and

The structure housing the Casa Loma stables and an extensive array of potting sheds was connected to the castle main house through an underground walkway. The stables and potting sheds were built during the period 1906–07, which was more than five years before the Pellatts were finally able to move into the big house, or what bedazzled Torontonians had come to know as Casa Loma. Interestingly, the walkway led to the building's huge heating plant (which incorporated a large Polson hot water boiler similar to the one used to generate steam on the Toronto Islands ferry *Trillium*) and a massive wine cellar.

During the years of the Second World War, the walkway allowed controlled access to a padlocked and highly secret experimental laboratory. It was in here that anti-submarine detection equipment, ASDIC, was being developed for the ships of the allied navies by staff of Toronto's Corman Engineering Co. As wartime tourists to the castle wandered through the walkway they probably never gave a thought to the sign on the laboratory door that read "Closed. Sorry for the inconvenience."

west ends of the castle and modify the main building, resulting in a total of fifty suites that would rent out for $4,000 per year (remember this is 1925). When the American plan didn't work out (interestingly a couple of years later Fuller went on to be a partner in the construction of the Empire State Building in New York City) local architect William Sparling entered the hotel business, and while the Casa Loma Hotel did open, the Great Depression soon ended it, along with other, much grander, projects.

In the fall of 1932, the city acquired the castle and property for $27,306 in back taxes. With ownership in hand, the city fathers called for tenders to demolish the building. It looked as if the end was in sight.

In the meantime, the Kiwanis Club of West Toronto obtained permission to operate the place on an interim basis as a tourist attraction. This "interim" period lasted for nearly eight decades.

The city is now working with the Liberty Entertainment Group (who run the Liberty Grand at the CNE along with the Rosewater and the Courthouse restaurants downtown) to develop plans to ensure the future of Toronto's castle as an exciting entertainment facility while recognizing Casa Loma as an important part of our city's history.

# Streetcar's Brush with Fame

## December 8, 2013

I first met Ken Kirsch a number of years ago when he contacted me seeking some assistance with a painting project he had in mind. No, he didn't want to paint one or two rooms in our house; rather, he was starting to turn a few old Toronto pictures into paintings. He had seen some views he particularly liked in some of my books that featured old photos of the city, and he wondered if I could I give him some history behind a few of the scenes, thereby making his work all the more interesting both for himself and for any potential customers. Turns out (and I didn't know this) Ken began his painting career at the age of eleven, eventually graduating in Graphic Design from Seneca College. He then worked in Eaton's Advertising Department and eventually with Gray Coach, a subsidiary of the TTC that provided inter-city and specialty motor coach service until phased out in 1990. Shortly thereafter Ken began his own graphic design company that soon merged with a large advertising agency. Now Ken had time to get back to his first love, painting scenes of an earlier, quieter, gentler Toronto. He had painted views of Muskoka, but views from Toronto's past remained Ken's favourite theme.

It wasn't long before his talents became well known through gallery shows and exhibitions as part of the McMichael Canadian Art Collection located in Kleinberg. People began asking Ken if he did commissioned works. One potential client was Syd Schatzker, who, like

The type of vehicle in all three images is the Presidents' Conference Committee (PCC) streetcar. From its introduction into the TTC fleet in 1938 until 1957, a total of 745 PCCs (new and used) were operated by the TTC, with the last such vehicle taken out of regular service on December 8, 1995. Two PCCs have been retained for special service. In this photo from the TTC Archives, PCC 4002, one of the first of the brand new vehicles to arrive in our city from the Montreal factory of Canadian Car and Foundry, is off-loaded at the TTC's Hillcrest Shops.

many Torontonians, had a fascination with Toronto's streetcars, especially the TTC's sleek art deco PCC Streamliners, the kind that many of us grew up with. Syd had found a view of PCC 4036 on the Internet and wondered if Ken could reproduce it in a painting, placing the streetcar in the exact same setting as in the photo.

Recalling my interest in Toronto's rich history, Ken asked if I could help him identify the intersection and add some additional historical details to enhance the final painting. The first thing that came to mind was that this particular streetcar, 4036, was part of the TTC's initial order for 140 similar vehicles, the first of which arrived in Toronto in 1938.

Then, using Google Maps, I was able to confirm that the streetcar (obviously on the Kingston Road route and in tripper or rush hour service) was turning south off Queen Street onto Parliament Street. (Incidentally,

Syd Schatzker was intrigued when he saw and subsequently bought this photo of Toronto streetcar 4036 that was offered for sale on the Internet. Little information accompanied the photo, but with a little detective work I was able to deduce the history of the streetcar, the location of the city intersection in the view, and, most interesting of all, the year and month the picture was snapped.

over the intervening half century the roof line in the background of both images has remained virtually unchanged). PCC 4036 would then proceed west on Front Street, perhaps to continue home to its carhouse at Roncesvalles and The Queensway via York and King streets.

The date of the original photo (and therefore Ken's painting) was a little more difficult until I examined with a magnifying glass the advertising cards on the front of the streetcar. Clue number one was the ad for Greenwood Raceway. It had been known since its opening in 1874 as Woodbine Racetrack. With the opening of New Woodbine in north Etobicoke, what had by then been renamed Old Woodbine became Greenwood Raceway.

On to clue number two. The second car card promoted the CNE's afternoon Grandstand Show, which would feature The Three Stooges (Moe, Larry, and the not-so-funny Curly Joe DeRita). Searching the CNE Archives' history site, I found that the trio appeared at the CNE on only one occasion, and that was during the period from August 20 to September 1, 1963.

Thornhill, Ontario, artist Ken Kirsch turned Syd's photo into this remarkable painting with one element of artistic license included. See what it is? The second streetcar has magically disappeared.

These two clues confirmed the date of the original photograph as sometime in the summer of 1963.

Oh, one last piece of Toronto streetcar trivia. Thanks to John Bromley's book Fifty Years of Progressive Transit, I discovered PCC 4036 was to have a special future following its retirement by the TTC in 1966. It would be one of 140 Toronto PCCs sold and shipped overseas to serve the streetcar riding public in Alexandria, Egypt. Sadly, this Toronto old-timer's ultimate fate is unknown.

# A Piece of T.O.'s Flying History

## December 15, 2013

In a recent column, I wrote about one of Toronto's little known airfields, Armour Heights. This week we visit another airport that remained in use by a flying club and several airline companies as late as 1931 and was the terminal for the first letters to be delivered by airplane ... although those letters were late in arriving.

Leaside Aerodrome, circa 1920. As the Great War staggered on, Great Britain was eager to have new aviators join the fledgling Royal Flying Corps (RFC). Many of these new pilots would be recruited in both Canada and the United States, where they received ground and flying instructions at various aviation schools located on both sides of the border. Locally there were facilities located at Hanlan's Point on Toronto Islands and at Long Branch in Etobicoke Township. In addition there were schools and flying fields at Armour Heights to the north of the city as well at the Leaside Aerodrome, which was established on a high plateau of land leased from the York Land Company to the east and south of the present busy intersection of Eglinton Avenue East and Laird Drive.

The new airfield, its lecture and mess halls, living quarters, and nine hangers were spread out over two hundred acres. Training began in 1917 and continued until war's end on November 11, 1918. Like most of the RFC's makeshift airfields, both Armour Heights and Leaside were subject to accidents, many of which were to result in fatalities. One such occurrence is highlighted on the gravestone of Lieutenant Wilfrid Tait, who rests in nearby Mount Pleasant Cemetery. The twenty-year-old Toronto-born aviator, along with Moose Jaw–born Second Air Mechanic Howard Belford, perished when the recently rebuilt engine in their JN-4 biplane suddenly burst into flames, causing the aircraft to plummet to earth in a ball of fire, not far from the recently laid out residential street named Aerodrome Crescent. What makes the accident even more tragic is the fact it happened on July 18, less than four months before the "war to end all wars" was finally over.

When the accompanying aerial photo was taken the grass covered airfield was no longer a military base but privately owned and operated until the early 1930s. The structure behind (south of) the hangers had originally been built by Canada Wire and Cable but was converted to produce munitions for the Allied troops during the Great War.

Four years after hostilities ended in late 1918 the building was acquired by the Durant Motor Company of Canada. This make of automobile was the brainchild of Billy Durant, the founder of General Motors, who was fired not once but twice by his company. Nothing daunted, Durant established a new company bearing his name south of the border in 1921. A variety of models were manufactured to compete with GM products. Sadly, Durant's new company went broke in 1931 with the Leaside factory coming under the ownership of the Dominion Motors name, where Canadian Frontenac cars and Rugby trucks continued to be built until the mid-1930s.

In 1934 the former ammunition factory turned automotive factory was again occupied by Canada Wire and Cable, that continued at the site until 1996 when it closed up operations in Leaside. The site was eventually cleared and is now the site of a sprawling shopping plaza.

Longo's new store in Leaside Village on Laird Drive near Millwood is located in the former Canadian Northern Railway's locomotive repair shop. The CNR had substantial holdings in the Leaside area and was folded into the government's new Canadian National Railways in the mid-1920s. This building was completed in 1919 and could service up to a dozen steam locomotives at one time. When the railway vacated the area for a new waterfront site in the late 1920s, this building became part of the E. S. & A. Robinson paper packaging factory (thus the name of the adjacent thoroughfare, Esandar Drive).

Vacant and boarded up for many years, a better fate awaited the sturdy structure. Instead of being demolished, as happens all too often in this country, the building has been sympathetically repurposed and is well worth a visit to see what can be done with our few remaining heritage buildings. Thanks, Longo's people.

# When Eaton's Was Christmas

## December 22, 2013

For many long-time Torontonians, the words *Christmas* and *Eaton's* go together like waffles and ice cream and donuts and an orange drink. For those who are newcomers to Canada or perhaps aren't old enough to remember Eaton's (or more correctly and officially the T. Eaton Company) it was for many, many years Canada's iconic department store.

Born in Ballymena, County Antrim, Northern Ireland in 1834 (interestingly the same year the Town of York became the City of Toronto), Timothy (who is the "T" in the company's official title) was just twenty when he immigrated to Canada West.

After trying his hand at several retail jobs around the province (which would be renamed Ontario with the creation of the new Dominion of Canada in 1867) Timothy moved to and opened a dry goods store at the southwest corner of the still relatively quiet Yonge and Queen intersection. It was here that in 1869 Torontonians Christmas shopped for the first time at Eaton's. Timothy had taken quite a gamble, since the shopping district of the day was along both sides of King Street east from Yonge and over to Jarvis.

In 1872 Timothy's new-found Scottish-born friend Robert Simpson (who was also born in Toronto's birth year) opened his own dry goods store on the north side of Queen Street directly opposite Eaton's emporium. For reasons unknown, the two entrepreneurs agreed to change

One of several buildings that made up the Eaton complex in the heart of the city was the Annex at the northwest corner of Albert and James streets. This ten-storey structure was built in the 1890s and was originally known as Eaton's House Furnishings Building. It was connected to the main store through a tunnel under the Albert and James Street intersection. Sometime in the 1930s it was renamed Eaton's Annex and soon became a sort of discount store, where when my brother and I were kids we went to get Bob a new pair of shoes. We took the noisy, old wooden escalator (Eaton's had the very first people mover of this kind in the entire country) up to the shoe department. On the way his beaten-up old running shoe got caught in the escalator's teeth and ripped the bottom out of one of the shoes. In an attempt to appease two rather self-conscious youngsters the manager of the department gave Bob a brand new pair. Can't recall whether we told Mom that we saved the $2 she had given us to buy new ones. We must have, right?

locations, a business decision that resulted in Simpson's occupying a store on the south side of the street and Eaton's on the north. (Simpson's was purchased by The Hudson's Bay Co. in 1978. Known for a time as simply The Bay, the company and the Queen Street store were recently renamed the Hudson's Bay Company.)

From 1869 and through the next 107 Christmases, the Eaton store continually expanded until by 1977 it occupied almost the entire Yonge, Queen, James, and Albert block. I say almost since many will remember the two-level Woolworth's store on the Yonge and Queen corner as well as a couple of small privately owned shops on the west side of Yonge Street north of Queen.

Then in 1977 Eaton's left its landmark store (which was subsequently demolished) and moved north to occupy a new store in the Eaton Centre. Eaton's declared bankruptcy in 1999.

Today all that's left of the once omnipresent Eaton name is the title of the Yonge Street shopping mall that along with the CN Tower and New City Hall has become a Toronto icon.

# 1944 Storm Still the Worst

## December 29, 2013

I can't help but feel badly for those of my fellow Ontarians who have suffered through a cold, snowy, and icy Christmas season and especially those who are still suffering. Our place in south Willowdale was without electricity for more than forty hours. As the hours passed, and being the tough Canadians we are, my wife, Yarmila, and I continued to add more and more layers of clothing even as the thermostat continued to drop.

And I'm quick to admit that in retrospect Yarmila was particularly clever to insist a couple of years ago that we convert our two wood fireplaces to natural gas. Over the hours, the one in the living room helped ward off at least some of the cold.

Another problem we had was the fact that our telephone was inoperative for almost as long as the electricity was out. I bought that ten-dollar corded phone just in case the cell network died. It didn't, but our darn landline did. That led to some particularly scary hours since it connected our place with our security company. They monitor break-ins and provide a fire detection service. So to wander too far was not a good idea. In fact, a nearby house caught fire, as did one on the street where I grew up in North Toronto. Did they subscribe to a security service, and were their landlines out as well?

Interestingly, when the electricity did come back on and lights began to glow brightly I felt much like those people who had gathered in Thomas Edison's workshop when his experimental lamp began to grow brighter and brighter. By the way, did you know that except for the outbreak of the so-called Mackenzie Rebellion back in 1837 Tom might have been a Canadian?

It was late in the afternoon of a snowy Tuesday, December 12, 1944, as the TTC's old wooden streetcar 1830 (built in 1912 in the old Toronto Railway's car building shop on Front Street at Princess) operating on the Beach route made its way east along Queen Street to its destination at the Bingham loop near Kingston Road and Victoria Park. It was packed with passengers, as many as 170, a police investigation later reported.

As the car approached the Mutual Street corner the operator failed to notice that the snow- and slush-covered switch that allowed streetcars access to the Mutual Street loop just north of the corner was in the curved position. It had not been reset. (Today, all streetcar operators who set manual switches to the "out of the normal" position are required to reset them before proceeding. In addition, all operators must check switch alignments before proceeding through intersections.) Travelling at a high rate of speed the old car "split the switch," lurched to one side, and tipped over. The big car slid for several yards north up Mutual, coming to rest on its right side straddling a huge mound of snow piled high as a result of what would go into the history books as the city's greatest ever accumulation of snow in a twenty-four-hour period, nearly two feet of the heavy white stuff.

That particular switch had been set in the curved position to allow one of the TTC's snow sweepers (similar to S-19 seen in the next photo) that had been eastbound clearing snow along Queen Street to reverse direction and continue clearing Queen in a westbound direction. While some pedestrians claimed that several of the modern PCC-type streetcars had proceeded through the switch without a problem, something had definitely gone wrong.

Of the 170 or so passengers on old 1830, a total of 43 required hospital treatment while one person succumbed to his injuries.

Now as I look out the window I see a convoy of Toronto Hydro trucks cruising the neighbourhood looking for and eager to help those who are still in the dark. Thanks, guys and girls. And thanks to those who've come in from out of town to help us.

Funny how you don't really miss things until you don't got 'em no more.

We've had a few serious wintertime storms that have caused trouble here in Toronto and environs. But to compare one with the other produces no meaningful conclusion. Copious quantities of ice battered our city in 1959 and again in 1968. The ice storm of 1998 was brutal for much of eastern Canada. But in terms of snow, what we do concede is that the almost two feet of the white stuff over a twenty-four-hour period in December 1944 still takes the cake. Now, having said that we still have four months to go before any possibility of heavy snow vanishes and it'll be safe once more to put my old 1955 Pontiac back on the road. Of course, the weather people were also sure that the December 1944 snowstorm would only be a few flurries.

TTC snow sweeper S-19, similar to the one involved in the streetcar derailment on December 12, 1944.

# Previously in the Toronto Sketches Series

**Toronto Sketches 11**
"The Way We Were"

Included in this eleventh compilation are stories about the controversial, though not altogether new, improvements to the TTC's St. Clair streetcar route, as well as accounts of such fondly remembered gasoline brands as Joy, B-A, and White Rose. Then there are those popular Great Lakes passenger ships that carried thousands to such "foreign" ports as Lewiston and Rochester in New York State. Recounting the unforgettable Toronto snowstorm of 1944 and the tragedy of the fire aboard the SS *Noronic* proves that not all memories are pleasant ones.

**Toronto Sketches 10**
"The Way We Were"

This tenth volume highlights some of Toronto's greatest landmarks such as the Don Jail and its graves and Hanlan's Point on Toronto Island. Mike also steps back in time to revisit the Avrocar, the flying saucer of the Great White North; takes a peek at Miss Toronto of 1926; conjures up The Hollywood, the city's first "talkie" theatre; and recalls historic snow days Canada's largest city has experienced.

# Also by Mike Filey

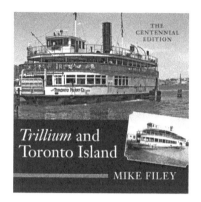

**Trillium and Toronto Island**
The Centennial Edition

The year was 1910 and signs of progress were in the air. That June, a new steam ferry for the Toronto Island Company was launched and christened the *Trillium*. Only briefly mentioned in the local dailies at the time, the double-end, side-paddled island ferry cruised the waters of Toronto Bay for nearly fifty years. After forty-six years of service, the *Trillium* retired in 1956, only to be saved from the scrap yard in 1973. The *Trillium* made its second debut in 1976 as a fully operational steam ferry and is still in service today.

As the *Trillium* reaches the century mark, Mike Filey revisits the history of this fascinating Canadian ship. With a new preface and updated photographs, including some in colour, Filey traces *Trillium*'s remarkable rise, fall, and rebirth in a book that honours one of Toronto's most interesting treasures.